Teacher and Student Behaviors

Teacher and Student Behaviors

Keys to Success in Classroom Instruction

Terrance M. Scott, Regina G. Hirn,
and
Justin T. Cooper

ROWMAN & LITTLEFIELD
Lanham • Boulder • New York • London

Published by Rowman & Littlefield
A wholly owned subsidiary of The Rowman & Littlefield Publishing Group, Inc.
4501 Forbes Boulevard, Suite 200, Lanham, Maryland 20706
www.rowman.com

Unit A, Whitacre Mews, 26-34 Stannary Street, London SE11 4AB

British Library Cataloguing in Publication Information Available

Library of Congress Cataloging-in-Publication Data Is Available

ISBN: 978-1-4758-2943-3 (cloth : alk. paper)
ISBN: 978-1-4758-2944-0 (paper : alk. paper)
ISBN: 978-1-4758-2945-7 (electronic)

Printed in the United States of America

Contents

List of Figures and Tables

FIGURES

TABLES

Preface

The information presented in this book is the result of a large-scale data collection effort at the University of Louisville between 2008 and 2015. Direct observation of teacher-student dyads in typical classrooms settings were collected across a range of schools and classrooms—elementary through high school, rural and urban, large and small, but with each observation focused on academic instruction (mathematics, reading/English, science, and social studies).

The original purpose was to create a snapshot of the average classroom from both a teacher and student perspective. But after nearly seven thousand such observations the snapshot took on more the feeling of a portrait. Analysis of age level, instructional grouping, academic content, number of adults in the room, and both teacher and student ethnicity and gender allows for a very rich look at both what instruction looks like in our public schools and how specific variables and behaviors mediate or predict student outcomes—both good and bad.

The interaction between the classroom teacher and a randomly selected target student was the dyad upon which all observations were focused. The rationale for observing a single random student was twofold in that it provided (1) the ability to designate demographic variables associated with an individual student (e.g., grade level, ethnicity) and (2) an index of typical interactions between the teacher and an individual student in the classroom.

Data were collected by trained observers who sat in the back of the room and used small hand-held devices to simply code teacher and student behaviors as they occurred. Because the focus of observation was on what happens during instructional time, observations began only when the teacher began instruction and lasted for fifteen minutes or until instruction stopped—whichever occurred first. Overall, interobserver reliability was assessed in more than 15 percent of observations. Reliability was calculated as the agreement of individual codes within a five-second window. The overall interobserver reliability was calculated at .98 across all codes.

Some behaviors were defined as simple occurrences and were recorded by tapping a label on the hand-held device. These "frequency codes" provide an index of the number of times a behavior occurred—converted to a rate per minute for comparison across all observations. Other behaviors were defined by the amount of time of occurrence and labels on the hand-held device initiated the starting and stopping of a timer for that behavior. These "duration codes" provide an index of the total amount of time in which the teacher or student engaged in a behavior—converted to a percentage of time for comparison across all observations.

The recording methods used in this study are common for this type of research and similar studies have been published over the past twenty years, albeit from much smaller and more focused samples. Typically data sets of two hundred observations from a single classroom would be considered large. In contrast, this eight-year study represents what is believed to be the largest database of its kind anywhere in the world. Although the clear majority of observations were collected from schools in Kentucky, the database also includes observations conducted in several other states and a small number collected from an elementary school in Sweden.

Since the beginning of this undertaking results have been examined in smaller chunks and published as descriptive analyses. In contrast, this book represents a larger and more sophisticated analysis of the full set of observation results. In addition, analyses of the impact of demographic variables and personal perceptions gleaned from the overall experiences of visiting such a large array of schools and classrooms is included. The intent is to provide the reader with an objective picture of the state of public school instruction and the degree to which we have the knowledge necessary to identify high-probability approaches to improving school outcomes.

The first chapter provides a rationale for considering specific teacher and student behaviors as a manner of assessing the effectiveness of instruction. Across all discussions the focus will remain on the degree to which teacher behaviors provide a probability for student success rates. To the extent that students are not sufficiently successful, the teacher must take responsibility for changing his or her behavior. The remaining chapters describe specific observed outcomes and discuss conclusions as to implications for how teacher behaviors may be altered to more reliably predict future student success.

Acknowledgments

The authors wish to acknowledge the enormous contributions of Marlene Parish, without whose assistance this research would not have been possible. Marlene has been the lead data collector and scheduler, responsible for training all data collectors and maintaining consistently high rates of interobserver reliability. Her commitment to excellence, organization, and professionalism are greatly appreciated by all involved.

In addition, we wish to acknowledge the dedication and professionalism of our core group of data collectors ("coders") that have been responsible for hundreds of hours of classroom observation over the years. Big thanks to Angela Dennis, Dana Hicks, Miriam Johnson, Cindy Rose, Ruth Teeple, and Denise Viola.

We also wish to acknowledge contributions by a range of friends and colleagues that have supported and contributed to our research efforts. First, thanks to Peter Alter, whose friendship and work was instrumental to getting the entire idea off the ground in the first place. Thanks to doctoral students Jon Burt, Beth Gurney, Nathan Havens, and Gwen Shultz for their suggestions during the development of the book and for contributing the questions at the beginning of each chapter. Thanks to Tim Lewis and Lee Kern for inviting us to work with them on a project that allowed us opportunities to refine and scale up the system we had in place. Thanks also to John Tapp for the dozens of communications to provide technical assistance with the technology. Finally, thanks to all of our families for their unending love and support.

Chapter One

A Logic for Evidence-Based Practices in Teaching and Learning

The sleep of reason produces monsters.

—Francisco Goya, 1797

GUIDING QUESTIONS

Teachers

1. What instructional methods lead to the largest student gains?
2. Between two instructional methods that work equally well (i.e., produces the same effect size) how do we decide between the two which to use?
3. Is teaching an art, a craft, or a science?

Administrators

1. District, state, and national standards often dictate what we must teach; by what criteria do you determine how you will teach the standards?
2. How much leeway should teachers be given to choose which pedagogical methods best suit them and their students?

Jimmy has been having difficulty in school. His reading level is below grade level and he often becomes defiant and belligerent when asked to participate. What's curious is that Jimmy is a very bright and capable student. Yet, small failures in reading early in his school career have grown, and teachers now report that he is too difficult to be involved with group instruction. Jimmy's case leaves us to wonder, is there anything that could have been differently in his schooling to have averted these behaviors and his failure with reading?

Why should we be concerned with whether a teacher uses one instructional practice instead of another or why a student is engaged or asking questions? Clearly, in at least some instances we believe that not all practices and behaviors are equal in terms of predicting success. This book is predicated on the notion that some instructional strategies are better than others—and that we have a pretty good idea of those teacher behaviors that provide the best probability for success. While the actual teacher and student behaviors upon which these observations focus are not novel, new, or technological, they do enjoy evidence of their superiority in terms of predicting successful student outcomes. Still, people in education do not always agree as to what constitutes evidence.

People tend to see themselves as unique enough that research cannot accurately predict what does and does not work for them personally (Mooney & Kirshenbaum, 2009). Clearly, people tend to find evidence to support what they believe—even in the face of highly contradictory evidence. This phenomenon is known as confirmation bias (Nickerson, 1998), and it affects both researchers and practitioners alike. When researchers ignore confirmation bias, they tend to see effects in their studies that aren't really there and when practitioners ignore confirmation bias, they tend to believe that their intervention practices work better than other things—even things they've never tried.

Curiously, the ability to develop one's personal truths with regard to evidence-based practice is somewhat peculiar to education among established professions. As professionals, physicians, engineers, architects, and pilots all subscribe to public truths in determining best practice. As a general rule, professionals in these and other similar fields do not ignore science in favor of their own idiosyncratic preferences. Bridge engineers don't buck science and decide upon their own version of what a span can hold. So why is this type of thinking acceptable in education?

Nineteenth-century logician Charles S. Pierce (1877) identified four methods of finding truth: (1) tenacity—ignore all other's views; (2) authority—views are forced and inquiry punished; (3) congruity—compromise to find agreement; and (4) scientific—inquiry that is fallible, tests itself, criticizes, corrects, and improves itself. Success, including social justice and equality, can only be protected by means of the last of these options. This chapter provides a basic model of considering evidence from a scientific viewpoint. It is this model that serves as the logic for selecting the teacher and student behaviors that are the focus of the nearly seven thousand observations.

To be clear, education should not be married to any strategy or philosophy for teaching. The teacher behaviors under consideration herein are simply those which provide the greatest evidence for making a positive difference with students. Should the evidence show in a believable way that some other teacher behaviors are more effective, then education as a field must be just as enthusiastic in pursuing those as best practice for teachers. As the English biologist Thomas Huxley has observed, science is "organized common sense where many a beautiful theory was killed by an ugly fact" (Stewart, 2008).

EVIDENCE-BASED PRACTICE

Let's begin this with a discussion of what it should mean to say that a teacher practice is *evidence-based*. Although the term seems fairly ubiquitous, the No Child Left Behind Act (2001) refers to practices that are proven effective by "scientifically based research" while other federal policy refers to practices that have been "proven to work" (US Department of Education, 2003). From within a medical model, evidence-based practice has been described as

> the conscientious, explicit and judicious use of current best evidence in making decisions about the care of the individual patient. It means integrating individual clinical expertise with the best available external clinical evidence from systematic research. (Sackett, 1996)

If we substitute *student* for *client* and *instructional* for *clinical* in this description it approaches what is proposed as consideration for the classroom as it provides for both the practice itself and the manner in which it is applied. That is, both the instruction and the teacher are a part of the practice.

For more than forty years, researchers have identified specific practices that are associated with positive student outcomes. Several recent books and special journal issues have discussed evidence-based practices in great depth (e.g., Graham, 2005; Scruggs & Mastropieri, 2009). From these reviews evidence-based practices generally consider the following three broad categories:

1. Arrangement of learning environments
2. Practices associated with the delivery of instruction (i.e., teaching)
3. Student outcomes

Teachers can arrange environments and provide instructions in a variety of ways but whether a practice is evidence-based will, in the end, be dependent upon what replicable and predictable effects it has on students.

Statistics and Believability

Realizing that studies can sometimes be wrong purely by random chance, education, as with most social sciences, has determined that evidence must statistically demonstrate that, if in fact there were no relationship, there is less than a 5 percent chance (0.05) of the seeing an effect of such size. When a study can demonstrate that this is the case the results are deemed to be *significant*. Assuming that a study is valid, statistical significance means that we believe that we have ruled out random chance to a reasonable degree. Other professions have higher standards for truth. For example, medicine typically uses one in a thousand (0.001).

For the sake of this discussion, let's say we are tossing a coin ten times and recording the number of heads and tails in each set of 10 (#heads-#tails). Now let's say we repeat this 10-set tosses of the coin a thousand times and plot the results as a frequency graph of heads-to-tails results from 0-10 through 10-0. What we'd find is that at the far right of the graph we'd see the few times that we saw ten heads and no tails (10-0) and at the far left of the graph we'd see the few times that we saw no heads and ten tails (0-10). In the middle of the graph would be the far more frequent outcomes 5-4, 5-5, and 4-5.

Consider the normal curve in figure 1.1. The divisions (standard deviations) help us to compare the results. The first standard deviation on either side of the mean always accounts for 34 percent of the population or 68 percent of the total population, and the second standard deviation accounts for another 14 percent on either side. This leaves only 4 percent of the population, and the third standard deviation accounts for approximately 1.96 percent on either side. Leaving only .08 percent of the population that are more than

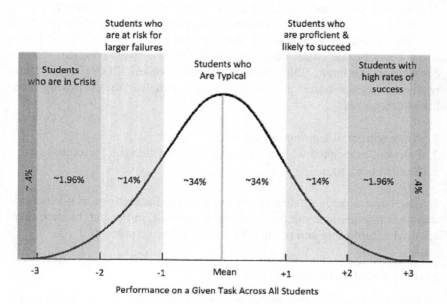

Figure 1.1   A Normal Distribution for Student Success Rates on a Given Task

three standard deviations above or below the mean. Standard deviations help us to put an individual outcome in perspective and to provide a standard by which to consider change.

When studies are conducted, statistical analyses are used to determine whether the observed results are different from what would be expected by chance. For example, consider a large jar filled with one hundred marbles. Five of those marbles are colored bright green and the rest are white. Thus, there is a 95 percent chance that dipping one's hand in and drawing a random marble will result in a white one. If an intervention allows one to randomly draw green marbles more than 5 percent of the time we could say that it is a statistically significant intervention (provides outcomes that are better than what would be expected by random chance).

To be certain, however, it is important to make sure that it wasn't a trick— that the green marbles are randomly mixed in, that all the marbles feel the same, and that the person demonstrating the intervention is not simply palming a green marble from the start. These safeguards are what we would call experimental control or issues of internal validity. They make the outcome believable.

When studies of educational intervention are published in reputable professional journals a panel of experts has carefully scrutinized the methodology, looking for such issues that might cause us doubt that what is being reported can be attributed solely to the intervention. But there are those who claim to do research and use it to sell training and products. While this in itself does not mean that these people are not honest, it should be a red flag in terms of believability. For evidence to be trustworthy we should attend to the following:

1. The evidence is based on empirical evidence and direct outcome measures—not on theory or perceptions.
2. The evidence is published in a peer-reviewed journal or other volume that has been approved by blind reviewers who carefully scrutinize the methods, analyses, and conclusions.
3. The authors of the study have no financial stake in the outcome of the study.
4. The evidence has been replicated by other researchers with similar results.
5. If the evidence is wildly different from the findings of other research on the same topic there are logical explanations as to why the differences were noted.

Evidence that does not meet all of these indicators may still be valid, but there is a need to be very skeptical and to demand further information. At what point should we be willing to believe that a given practice warrants our trust as the best course of action? To answer this we need to know more than just whether it works, we need to know whether it works better than other things.

Comparative Effects

Consider that an important task is to move a bean from one side of the room to the other. It will be considered a success if the bean ends up across a line drawn near the far wall. To study the problem a researcher on his hands and knees and began pushing the bean with his nose. After careful study it was found that the bean did get closer to the finish line as a result of this action so the researcher wrote a grant proposal and was funded to further study this intervention.

Next, a very tightly controlled study was created wherein twenty people worked on moving the bean across the room with their noses and another twenty attempted to move the bean but without touching it—all while a research team measured the distance of bean movement each day. After some statistical analysis the results were accepted in a peer-reviewed research journal and other researchers subsequently replicated the study with the same result. It can be said that research has now concluded that nose-pushing is an evidence-based practice for the moving of beans across a room, because it has met all of our criteria.

Looking at this logically, it is obvious that just because people can move a bean across the room with their nose does not mean there is not a better way to do it. If all we really want is for the bean to be moved then what about carrying it or throwing it? It certainly seems like those strategies would offer the same result—or better, and with less time and effort. Clearly, we can't judge the worth of a practice solely by the effect.

We also have to be concerned with comparisons—are there things that work better? For example, two math interventions both produce the same result, one within one week and the other in one month. Although the end result was the same, these are equivalent interventions. Similarly, two behavior interventions are successful in getting students to meet the desired criterion of handling frustrations with appropriate verbalizations during 80 percent of opportunities by the end of the month. However, one of the interventions saw effects averaging 80 percent while the other produced effects of better than 90 percent in the same period. Although both met the goal within the timeline, one appears to be more effective than the other.

One mechanism we have for comparing interventions is to look at the effect size. The effect size is a calculation of how much change occurs as a result of intervention. Recall our discussion of standard deviation. An effect size describes the amount of change that occurs in the result of an intervention.

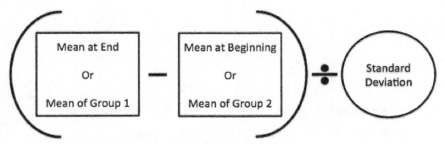

Figure 1.2   The Basic Formula for Computing an Effect Size

That is, if the standard deviation on some outcomes we were measuring ended up being 10 points, then an intervention demonstrating an average effect of 10 points could be said to have an effect size of 1 (i.e., one standard deviation). The formula for this is presented in figure 1.2.

Let's take an example of two math interventions focused on student ability to perform long division (figure 1.3 presents a graphic representation of this example). These are being conducted by two different research teams and measured with two different long-division assessments. The first intervention, M1, is being measured with assessment A1. Assessment A1 has a mean of 100 and a standard deviation of 15. The second intervention, M2, is being measured with assessment A2, which has a mean of 120 and a standard deviation of 20. Hundreds of participating students have been assessed and were found to be right at the mean in both studies.

After interventions M1 and M2 are completed the students are assessed again and the results show significant gains for students in both interventions. The average score for M1 is 110 points, indicating a growth of 10 points with assessment A1. The mean score of M2 is 130, also indicating a growth of 10 points with assessment A2. The effect size of M1 is calculated at $110 - 100/15 = .67$ and for M2 it is calculated at $130 - 120/20 = .5$. But don't get hung up on the math part of it because it's just the logic that is important (and all we did was divide). Although both might be evidence-based practices, M1 has a larger effect size even though the actual gains were equal.

The effect size is useful in comparing the interventions because it provides information not only on whether the effect was significant but also on how big the effect was. Assume that we have two interventions, both with strong research demonstrating significant statistical effect. We know they both work but, is one better than the other? One answer to this question is strictly related to efficiency. Did one intervention produce the effect with less time and effort?

The way to make comparisons is to look at effect sizes. Both worked to criterion and did so within a week—but a larger effect size for one shows that

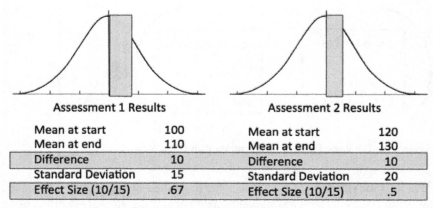

Assessment 1 Results		Assessment 2 Results	
Mean at start	100	Mean at start	120
Mean at end	110	Mean at end	130
Difference	10	Difference	10
Standard Deviation	15	Standard Deviation	20
Effect Size (10/15)	.67	Effect Size (10/15)	.5

Figure 1.3   Comparing Effect Sizes across Two Effective Interventions

it typically provides a bigger larger effect. Of course, issues of effect and efficiency need to be balanced out. Clearly, the intervention that is far more expen-
sive and time consuming is worth more when the effect is much larger. But when
the effects are very close in size, a more efficient intervention may be preferable.

HIGH-PROBABILITY BEHAVIORS IN
TEACHING AND LEARNING

When considering how we might best affect student success the question is
what strategy or set of strategies provides the best probability for increasing student performance. In figure 1.4 assume that A represents a student
(or a classroom full of students) and C represents some outcomes that we
consider to be representative of success. Thus, C might be that students pre-
dictably say "4" when queried about a problem of $2 + 2$, or handle a conflict
without physical violence. The p represents the probability of the student
actually demonstrating that successful outcome. Knowing the student(s)
and the expected outcome, it is possible to plug in possible interventions
under B and compare to see which provide the highest probabilities for
success.

High-Probability Teacher Behaviors (Large Effect Sizes)

Looking at the whole of the research base with regard to effective instruction,
a short list of critical and foundational teacher behaviors are illuminated as
providing the highest probability for student success. Clearly, however, there

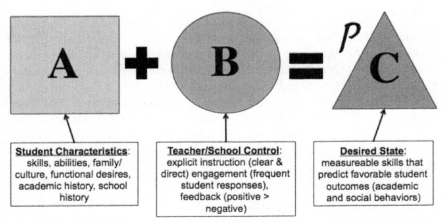

Figure 1.4   The Probability Equation for Predicting Success where *P* = the Probability of a Successful Outcome

is no single best way of providing these foundational practices. Teachers must assess student needs in the context of the desired curricular goals and create instruction that includes the best mix of evidence-based practices.

Explicit Instruction

Instruction is most effective when delivered in a clear, direct, and explicit manner (Kirschner, Sweller, & Clark, 2006). Effective teachers break content into teachable components and then model and demonstrate key rules to maximize the probability of student understanding. While this can be difficult to measure via direct observation, available research has focused on the degree to which teachers engage with the instructional content as they lead a lesson.

Engagement

In contrast to the teacher's engagement with the lesson content, there is no greater predictor of student success than the degree to which the student was engaged with the instructional content during the lesson (Berliner, 1990). But the student's engagement is dependent upon the teacher's ability to encourage and promote it. That is, there are specific teacher behaviors that enhance student engagement. In a general sense, teacher behaviors that promote student engagement are referred to as teacher-presented, student opportunities to respond (OTR). Counts of these teacher behaviors are the most frequent index of the degree to which teachers encourage student engagement.

Feedback

Regular feedback is a critical component of instruction. In fact, it's difficult to conceive of how one could teach a new skill without letting the students know whether their performance is correct. However, feedback is most effective when there is more positive than negative (Brophy, 2006). This cannot be achieved simply by decreasing negative feedback as students must know when an error has been made. Rather, teachers must design instruction in a way that creates more student success—and thus more opportunities for positive feedback. Feedback is generally assessed as both a frequency and a ratio of positive to negative.

Other Variables and Mediating Variables

While explicit instruction, engagement, and feedback can be considered the foundational components of effective instruction there are other important variables that may also have a large impact—although they often defy clear measurement. Teacher-student relationships, arrangement of the instructional environment, and consistency all have strong evidence supporting effect. However, each is difficult to judge as part of a short-term observation. The lack of a focus on these variables here should not be taken as dismissive of their importance. Rather, direct observations are better suited to more discrete teacher and student behaviors.

It is also possible that an endless array of other possible variables might mediate the effect of the identified teacher behaviors. For example, feedback rates may have differential effects with elementary versus high-school students, in math versus reading, or in small groups versus whole classrooms. While there is little existing evidence for such differential effects, a range of potentially mediating variables including ethnicity and race of student and teacher, group size, academic content, and number of teachers in the room have been collected and will be discussed.

High-Probability Student Behaviors

Although the focus of the observations discussed herein will be squarely on the teacher's role in effective instruction, student behavior is also reported for a couple of reasons. First, student behavior is the outcome by which teacher effectiveness is ultimately determined. Because student active engagement is perhaps our best index of achievement, in the absence of longer term achievement data active engagement can be used to judge the effectiveness of teacher practices. Second, teacher and student behaviors are reciprocal in nature—one affecting the other. Knowing whether a student is engaged, off task, or disruptive provides for some interesting analyses with regard to how student behavior is a predictor for teachers' use or abandonment of effective practice.

Chapter Two

What Goes on in Typical Classrooms?

The belief that all genuine education comes about through experience does not mean that all experiences are genuinely or equally educative.

—John Dewey

GUIDING QUESTIONS

Teachers

1. How do I compare to the "typical" teacher described in this study?
2. How can I improve my teaching and thus outcomes for my students?

Administrators

1. How do the students and teachers in my school compare to the students and teachers in this study?
2. What should our focus be for each group to improve outcomes at our school?

Although all of the people working on this project had extensive experience as classroom teachers and had continuously worked in a variety of schools throughout their careers, no one was quite sure what the data from this large-scale observation would show. We all had in our mind a picture of what classrooms look like—and believed the mean was generally somewhere between the rigid teacher-controlled lessons portrayed on television shows such as *The Andy Griffith Show* in the 1960s and the more student-centered classrooms exemplified by the Montessori model.

13

We'd all seen a number of teachers across a range of schools: urban and rural, large and small, rich and poor, high and low achieving, with and without chronic behavior problems, and serving ages from early childhood through high school. However, this broad range of experiences in some ways hampered our ability to determine what "normal" looked like—or what precise behaviors constitute a typical lesson. While the low rates of effective instructional behaviors described in the following chapters did not surprise us, we admit to being shocked by the degree to which effective practices were neglected as a part of instruction in the typical classroom.

Ideally, we would have seen teachers that dedicated every minute of instructional time to the lesson at hand, found ways to engage students at very high rates throughout the lesson, and provided continuous feedback to students who were generally successful better than 80 percent of the time. In reality, none of these things are occurring in the typical classroom. As we expected, classrooms typically fall somewhere between the TV caricature extremes. But regardless of whether classroom teachers were rigid or loose in their approach, instruction generally involved very low rates of teacher attention and equally low rates of student engagement and enthusiasm.

THE TYPICAL OBSERVATION

The majority of observations were collected as part of schoolwide assessment. That is, we entered the school in the morning and systematically worked to observe every classroom teacher for fifteen minutes during core content instruction. Often teachers had students in laboratory settings, independent work, or other contexts that did not include an actual lesson. Under these circumstances observers returned the next day to find a better time to complete the observation. Thus, given three to four observers and overlap for interobserver reliability, a typical school observation took two to three days to complete.

Typical Schools

A full range of schools was observed as a part of this project. Table 2.1 provides a summary of observation counts by school level and type. Each of the total of 6,752 refers to a single observation of a teacher-student dyad in that school. For example, there have been 3,126 unique teacher-student dyads observed in elementary school classrooms and 174 of the same in alternative school classrooms. Because observation counts in P–K, K–8, K–12, middle-high, and alternative schools are all much lower, results herein are reported only for elementary, middle, and high schools.

Table 2.1   **Number of Observations by School Level and Type**

School Level and Type	Number of Observations
P–K	30
Elementary	3,126
Middle	1,127
High	1,844
Middle/high	174
K–8	222
K–12	55
Alternative	174

While alternative school classrooms are not included in the lager analyses because of relatively low observation totals, these schools were among the most interesting in terms of both teacher and student behaviors. As one might expect, alternative schools had the highest number of student disruptions. What might not be expected is, anecdotally, these schools also had the highest number of teachers who outright refused to allow observers in their classrooms. Even after being told by the principal that observations were required, multiple teachers in one alternative school locked their doors and ignored observer requests to enter.

Observers also returned from alternative schools with rich and sometimes alarming stories. Observers in these schools were the target of direct insults, obscene taunts, and even pencils thrown. In addition, they were exposed to student-on-student assaults, arrests, school lock down, and on one occasion a schoolwide search by drug sniffing dogs. While this is certainly not the norm in other schools, occasional verbal abuse by students in regular middle and high schools was not uncommon. In at least two regular schools observers asked not to return as they did not feel safe.

School Environment

The school environment can be described in a variety of ways. Contemporary vernacular for this construct includes learning environment, climate, and culture. No formal or informal measures of environment were collected as part of the observation protocol. Rather, we consider environment in terms of both teacher/student behaviors and observers' anecdotal reports.

While we did not collect observers' anecdotal information in any systematic manner and thus have no manner of assessing more qualitative perceptions, observers who worked across schools claim to be able to predict observation outcomes based on a general feeling in the school. They report that schools where the principal provided a clear observation schedule and helped to facilitate observations were more likely to have teachers engaging in effective instructional practices. In contrast, schools where principals were aloof, unhelpful, or unseen tended to have lower observed levels of effective instruction among teachers.

Again, we have no hard data to support these perceptions, but observers further reported that the degree to which a school was clean, organized, and friendly also tended to have teachers that used higher rates of effective instructional behaviors and students that were more engaged and less disruptive. There are two issues that arise from these reports. First, it is possible that these perceptions to some degree drive how observers interpret teacher behaviors. In other words, observers see teachers as being more effective when the environment is appealing. However, all observation variables were concrete and interobserver agreement was overall at or above 90 percent for all teacher and student variables.

Second, if there is a connection between the environment and teacher/student behaviors, what is the nature of that connection? Do organized and friendly environments enhance the use of effective instruction or is it the other way around? Perhaps effective instruction produces higher rates of success among both teachers and students that play a role in creating a more positive environment. While there is no way to further assess this issue from the data we have, the question is interesting and worthy of future consideration. Of course, it's also possible that the perceived connection is simply in the mind of the observers.

Typical Classrooms

Academic Content Focus

Observations took place only during academic instructional times in classrooms focused on academic content. Across all schools observed, reading or language arts made up the largest percentage of observations. Because observers randomly selected observation times and rooms, this is evidence that reading and other language arts including English and foreign language instruction is the content area upon which classroom focus most of their time—especially at the elementary level where reading, spelling, and associated language arts make up 63 percent of all observed instruction. The total number of observations across content areas is presented in table 2.2, and a summary of content-area instruction across all observations is presented by grade level in table 2.3.

Mathematics is a distant second in elementary but a close second in middle and high schools where reading and language arts focus is decreased. Interestingly, science and social studies each make up only 5 percent of instructional time. Even at middle and high school neither subject area

Table 2.2   Number of Observations by Content Area

Reading/Language Arts	Mathematics	Science	Social Studies
3,748	1,772	547	685

Table 2.3   Mean Percentage of Observation Time by Content Area and School Level

	Elementary (%)	Middle (%)	High (%)
Reading/language arts	63	34	41
Mathematics	27	30	34
Science	5	19	9
Social studies	5	18	16

accounts for more than 19 percent, with science still only being observed 9 percent of the time in high school. Assuming that 1,844 random high-school observations reveal what typically occurs in these classrooms, science appears to receive relatively little time. Perhaps this is because it is not a part of typical states' assessment and thus not as important to teachers.

Multiple Adults Involved with Instruction

Observers recorded whether there was more than one adult involved with instruction in the classroom. Additional adults in the classroom were not recorded if they were not involved with instruction by assisting the teacher in engaging students or delivering content. Table 2.4 provides a summary of additional adult participation in the classroom by school level. Note that additional adults are most common at elementary and decreases across middle and high school.

Recording information on adult involvement with instruction consisted solely of noting more than one and did not provide information on whether that number was two or higher. Further, there is no information available as to the nature of any additional adults. For example, we cannot say whether these persons were collaborative special education teachers, student teachers, or educational assistants. In addition, when more than one adult were involved with instruction all of their behaviors were recorded as teacher behavior.

Table 2.4   Percentage of Classrooms by School Level with More than One Adult Providing Instruction

Elementary (%)	Middle (%)	High (%)
17.9	15.1	10.6

Thus, if two adults each provided a feedback statement to a student it was recorded as two teacher behaviors.

Typical Teachers

As human beings, teachers present a complexity that defies definition of typical. However, we can define teachers by some basic demographic and behavioral features that allow us to paint a picture of what observers typically saw when observing teachers. After thousands of observations the picture of a typical teacher begins to emerge—but that picture varies by school level. As a general rule, effective instructional practices decrease from elementary to middle school and again from middle school to high school. In addition, although the variance is generally not great, examples at both ends of the spectrum have been seen.

First, teachers at all levels are more likely to be female. This is most pronounced at the elementary level where more than 92 percent of observed teachers were female. However, by high school the numbers have mostly evened out. In terms of ethnicity, nonwhite persons made up slightly less than 7 percent of observed teachers at the elementary and middle school levels, increasing to 12.7 percent at the high-school level. At best, these rates are still less than half of what would be expected if nonwhite teachers were proportional to their prevalence in the communities in which observations were made. Table 2.5 summarized teacher demographic information.

In general, extreme performances (low and high) tended to disproportionately affect the mean. For example, across 1,844 high-school observations the mean high school level of "teaching" was 72 percent, with 669 instances of 100 percent and only 7 instances of 0 percent—meaning that 63.3 percent of observations fell between the extremes and 36 percent were accounted for by the positive extreme. In contrast, the mean rate of positive feedback among high-school teachers was 0.033 with 1,317 instances of 0 and 2 instances of 11 (highest observed frequency)—meaning that only 28.4 percent fell between the extremes and 71 percent were accounted for by the low extreme.

It was our general belief going in that our results would reflect a best-case scenario for teacher practices. First, observations occurred only during the first fifteen minutes of instruction—during the time when the teacher is providing directions and interacting with student to set up more independent

Table 2.5   Percentage of NonWhite and Male Teachers by School Level

	Elementary (%)	Middle (%)	High (%)
Nonwhite teachers	6.9	6.7	12.7
Male teachers	7.8	28	48

performance. We continue to believe that observing bell-to-bell would result in much lower rates of instructional behaviors as it would include transitions, taking roll, and overseeing independent practice. Observing only during fifteen minutes beginning at the start of teacher instruction provides an inflated picture of teacher practice rates.

Considering that teachers knew what we were looking for during observations, we also believed that teachers would react to our presence and exhibit higher rates of behavior than would otherwise be the case. While it is not possible to truly know whether this is the case, the number of observations during which not a single engagement or feedback statement was observed leads us to believe that there was far less reactivity than anticipated. It is not clear, however, whether this means that teachers believe their typical rates are sufficiently high as is, don't adequately understand what the target behaviors are, or simply don't care.

Of course there were egregious examples of noninstruction with teachers simply sitting at their desks and occasionally providing a random direction. One high-school teacher was observed talking to students from her desk and behind a newspaper for the entire observation period, for instance, and many observations were discarded because the teacher did not provide instruction, having students work independently at their desks throughout the period. But these were largely the exception rather than the rule and the great majority of teachers seemed to be genuinely concerned with the students' attention and the delivery of effective instruction.

Typical Students

Like teachers, students are a complex and diverse group than can be typified only by concrete demographics and observed behaviors. In order to insure random selection of students, observers created selection criteria prior to entering a classroom. For example, the observer might determine that the target student would be the one closest to the teacher or whoever was sitting in the first row third seat.

Given random selection, the disproportionately high numbers of minority students and males observed at the high school are of concern. First, we assume that the high schools in which we observed were over-representative of those in areas with significantly higher numbers of nonwhites. However, most observed elementary and middle schools were in the same neighborhoods as the high schools we observed and show numbers that approximate the community. In terms of gender inequities at the high school we do not have an explanation as proportions at elementary and middle school fall out as we would expect. Table 2.6 summarizes demographic information for students.

Table 2.6 Percentage of NonWhite and Male Students by School Level

	Elementary (%)	Middle (%)	High (%)
Nonwhite students	34	25	52.4
Male students	52.8	49.1	60.2

Student Engagement

The typical student was on task and attending to the lesson in some way. At elementary and middle school, students were passively engaged (watching the teacher or attending as directed) most of the time, with active engagement taking the lead by high school. However, active engagement was defined for students as participating physically—reading, writing, building, discussing, demonstrating, and so on. By high school we begin to see more worksheets and independent work that, while meeting our definition of active engagement, is not really what we had in mind for this category.

There is a definitional problem when students working alone on a worksheet are coded as actively engaged in the same way as a student building a model while discussing with peers. Students working alone and with only occasional teacher monitoring may be engaged but this certainly is not the same as having discussions and immediate feedback. While students in high school are more likely to be actively engaged by this definition, they are also more likely to be off task. Thinking backward we now see that off-task rates are likely elevated as a result of higher rates of worksheet style work.

Shortly after our first pilot observation sessions we realized that there were not always clearly delineated tasks or engaging opportunities for students. That is, if the student is not doing anything—but the teacher has not asked him or her to do anything, the observer cannot determine whether the student is on or off task. For these situations we developed a code for "downtime" that is used when there is no obvious expectation as part of the lesson. Downtime is actually more of a teacher behavior than a student behavior but we've included it here because it still describes typical student engagement.

Because of these issues with defining active engagement, off task is perhaps a better index of how student engagement changes across school levels. The average elementary student is off task only 3.3 percent of the time, growing slightly to 4.5 percent by middle school. However, at high school off task more than doubles to 11.6 percent. Pair this with 5.5 percent downtime and the average high-school student is disengaged from instruction 17.1 percent of the time. Considering this in light of the fact that high-school teachers provide no instruction 28 percent of the time (see chapter 3) and the problems with the quality of instruction at this level is clear. Table 2.7 summarizes student engagement levels.

Table 2.7   Percentage of Time Students Engaged during Instruction by School Level

	Elementary (%)	Middle (%)	High (%)
Actively engaged	39.1	41.7	43.4
Passively engaged	54.9	49.9	39.5
Off task	3.3	4.5	11.6
Downtime	2.7	3.9	5.5

Hand-Raising and Teacher Acknowledgment

As observers sat in classrooms surrounded by a full array of students and behaviors they recorded only those behaviors of a randomly selected target student. Because data was collected in this way we are able to make statements about what the typical student receives from the teacher—and also what the typical teacher receives from a typical student. Student hand-raising and the teacher's subsequent acknowledgment of the raised hand is an example of such reciprocal behaviors.

Student hand-raising decreases as school level increases—starting at 0.225 times per minute at elementary and decreasing to 0.109 times per minute by high school. But teachers typically acknowledge students with raised hands during only 41 percent of instances in elementary school. Of particular interest is the fact that teachers tend to acknowledge hand-raising at a fairly stable rate across grade levels (0.08 to 0.094 times per minute) regardless of how often students raise their hand. Perhaps this is why student hand-raising decreases over the years—they learn that it will not work. Table 2.8 summarizes student hand-raising and teacher acknowledgment.

We have found the results of the hand-raising and acknowledgment to be among the most perplexing findings. Across every grade-level teachers consistently remind student to raise their hands to get attention and complain that student talk-outs are a major source of frustration. At the same time, if teachers do not provide attention for raised hands there is little reason for students to continue. Assuming that the purpose of both hand-raising and disruptions are to get teacher attention, lack of

Table 2.8   Rate per Minute of Student Hand-Raising and Teacher Acknowledgment of Raised Hand (Percentage of Hand Raises Acknowledged) by School Level

	Elementary	Middle	High
Student hand-raising	0.225 (1 per 4.44 minutes)	0.138 (1 per 7.25 minutes)	0.109 (1 per 9.17 minutes)
Teacher acknowledgment	0.094 (41%)	0.08 (58%)	0.08 (73%)

Table 2.9   Rate per Minute of Disruptive Behavior by School Level (Once Every X Minutes)

Elementary	Middle	High
0.03	0.03	0.058
(1 per 33.33 minutes)	(1 per 33.33 minutes)	(1 per 17.24 minutes)

acknowledgment for hand-raising incentivize disruptions that are much harder for the teacher to ignore.

Disruptive Behavior

Disruption was coded when a student displayed behavior that did or potentially could have interrupted the lesson in such a way that it distracted the teacher and/or other students (e.g., out of seat, makes noises, talks to peer, makes loud comments, and makes derogatory comments). Disruptive behaviors ranged from low intensity (distracting another student by whispering) to high intensity (making threatening statements or destroying property). Disruption can be identified by volume, threatening words, derogatory, or physical disruption. The rate of disruptive behaviors by grade level is presented in table 2.9.

Continuing a general trend, disruptions occur much more frequently in high school than in either elementary or middle school. The rates of observed disruptions reported here are in reference to a single average student. Multiply this by all students in the classroom and the rates are more alarming. For example, the average high-school student is disruptive once every 17.24 minutes. Multiply this by twenty students in a classroom and it becomes clear that an average high-school teacher may typically be exposed to nearly seventy disruptions per hour. However, because observed rates of negative feedback from high school show that teachers provide such feedback only about once every twenty-one minutes (see chapter 5), most disruptions are being ignored.

INTEROBSERVER RELIABILITY

All observers were trained using a protocol described in the Classroom Observation Training Manual, which is included as an appendix. Observers were trained using video and supported in vivo observations and were required to meet a minimum interobserver agreement with the trainer before conducting solo observations. Interobserver reliability was collected during 15 percent of all observations by having two observers code separately.

Table 2.10   Interobserver Reliability Coefficients by Observation Codes

Observation Code	Code Type	Reliability Coefficient
Opportunity to respond—group	Frequency	.93
Opportunity to respond—individual	Frequency	.89
Student hand-raising	Frequency	.91
Teacher acknowledgment of hand-raising	Frequency	.91
Teacher direction	Frequency	.94
Positive feedback	Frequency	.90
Negative feedback	Frequency	.93
Correction	Frequency	.85
Student disruption	Frequency	.93
Teacher teaching (curricular/student engagement)	Duration	.99
Teacher not teaching (no curricular/student engagement)	Duration	.99
Whole-group instruction	Duration	1.00
Small-group instruction—peers	Duration	1.00
Small-group instruction—teacher	Duration	1.00
Independent work	Duration	.99
One-to-one instruction	Duration	1.00
Downtime	Duration	1.00
Off task	Duration	1.00
Passive engagement	Duration	.98
Active engagement	Duration	.98

The MOOSES® (Tapp & Wehby, 1995) data collection software used for all observations also calculated interobserver reliability using a five-second window for agreement by code. Reliability coefficients for the all variables ranged from .85 to 1.00. A full summary of interobserver reliability by code is presented in table 2.10.

SUMMARY

Throughout the following chapters we continue to present results in terms of the average classroom, average teacher, and average student. While there are inherent limitations to looking at students in isolation rather than at entire classrooms, after 6,752 observations of every classroom in a school and randomly selected students we have great capacity for describing what is typical. Chapters 3 through 5 discuss observations with regard to specific teacher and student behaviors while chapter 6 looks at the evidence for differential effects and mediating variable in considering how observed of what is typical might be explained.

Chapter Three

Instruction

Teacher Presentation, Use of Directions, and Instructional Grouping

Do the difficult things while they are easy and do the great things while they are small.

—Lao Tzu

GUIDING QUESTIONS

Teachers

1. What components make teaching most effective?
2. How does my teaching compare to most effective strategies, and what can I change to become more effective?

Administrators

1. Which teachers in my building seem to follow the model of most effective teaching?
2. What coaching or professional development can I implement to improve the teaching of my faculty that need remediation?

While there are factions within the field of education that might argue the point, in general, there is no debate that instruction is the heart and soul of teaching. Instruction can be broadly defined as the set and sequence of behaviors in which the teacher engages to increase student success. Anyone can simply tell students what to do, and it takes no thought or skill to allow students to explore with hopes of learning on their own. Teachers not only convey information, but they also engage in behaviors and strategies that increase the probability that the students will be successful. This is what we call instruction.

This chapter is focused on teacher behaviors during the delivery of instruction. When thinking about instructional delivery, the teacher must consider the student's prior knowledge, the content to be learned, and what materials and procedures will be needed to optimize the lesson. Clearly, an understanding of the content is critical to an effective lesson; however, understanding what is to be taught is just a beginning step in the instructional design process. This necessarily involves some careful considerations on the part of the teacher for each unique lesson in terms of what specific teacher behaviors are indicated and how they should be sequenced.

Let us begin this peek into classrooms with a discussion of "teaching" at a most simplistic level. Teaching includes the demonstration or description of a term, concept, procedure, or topic. Teaching might include examples, visuals, experiments, or an experience providing students critical information for learning. At the very minimum, "teaching" includes supervision of students as they complete an activity—providing feedback and negotiating classroom management. "Students achieve more in classes where they spend most of their time being taught or supervised by their teachers rather than working on their own (or not working at all)" (Brophy & Good, 1986, p. 361).

In the classroom, teachers use established lessons that have been specifically developed to convey content to students. Lesson designs are typically chosen through individual teacher selection or school/district mandate. For example, a school may require the use of a lesson design template providing prompts for connections to standards, objectives, activities, and assessment procedures. In contrast, teachers may be allowed to construct all or part of the lesson design on their own within given general parameters. Either format requires the teacher to consider basic instructional components as lessons are developed.

EXPLICIT INSTRUCTION

While the exact nature of lesson design may vary across content areas, a core of explicit and systematic instruction provides a foundation for all teaching (Kirschner, Sweller, & Clark, 2006; Vaughn, Gersten, & Chard, 2000). Direct instruction is a science-based process for delivering explicit instruction and involves an array of teacher behaviors that drive instruction in a manner that maximizes student success (Engelmann, 2007). These teacher behaviors are sometimes referred to as part of an instructional sequence—the specific behaviors indicated for a given lesson.

With a focus on maximizing student success, sequences of instructional behaviors have been developed for use with particular populations of learners. For example, the National Mathematics Advisory Panel (2008) describes explicit instruction as a preferred practice for improving mathematics performance among students identified as low achieving or with learning disabilities. In the area of literacy, instructional sequences involve direct and explicit teaching of phonics, vocabulary, and text comprehension strategies (National Institute for Literacy, 2001). For behavior, a recommended teaching instructional sequence for students identified with behavioral concerns includes the use of questions or requests, feedback, and active engagement (Gunter, Denny, Jack, Shores, & Nelson, 1993).

Explicit instruction refers to instructional sequences that include review, direct presentation of content material in an engaging manner, teacher-facilitated and guided practice, consistent feedback, and independent practice (Roshenshine & Stevens, 1986). It is direct in its approach to teaching—maximizing the probability of student success with the content. Explicit instruction is based on the scientific principles of effective teaching and learning, including the promotion of student success by encouraging time engaged with content and carefully considering instructional groupings to provide ample structure and guidance for varied skill levels (Ellis & Worthington, 1994).

Explicit instruction can also be considered in terms of teacher clarity, or the degree to which the teacher is able to get his or her points across to the students. Teacher clarity includes key components of the explicit systematic instructional model and was included in Hattie's (2009) ranking as a top ten contributor to student success. Importantly, clarity is enhanced through the same teacher behaviors described as part of explicit instruction: organization, explanation, provision of examples, guided practice, and assessment of student learning (Fendick, 1990).

Unfortunately, educators often respond to the tenets of explicit instruction with concern or even dread. This negative perception may be the result of a poor experience with an instructional product, lack of training on the key components of the instruction model, or lack of practice with key features. In addition, direct and explicit instruction is often eschewed by teacher training programs as passé, or worse, as ineffective. In reality, research continues to support explicit instruction as the most effective method of maximizing student success and confidence, especially among students with a history of failures (e.g., Brophy & Good, 1986; Rivkin, Hanushek, & Kain, 2005).

Effective teachers break concepts and skills into teachable components through modeling and demonstration, provide clear and detailed instructions, ask questions to determine understanding, and provide practice with guidance and feedback (Rosenshine, 1986). This chapter provides a closer look at teacher behaviors as sequences of instruction. Classroom observations described in this chapter provide a glimpse of teacher behaviors within this sequence through calculation of time spent teaching (e.g., demonstrating or modeling), rate of directions provided to students, and use of instructional grouping during instruction.

TIME TEACHING

For the purpose of this discussion, "time teaching" is defined as the percentage of time in which teachers were observed modeling, demonstrating, or providing verbal or written examples, or simply looking at the students. This definition is not meant to define what it means to "teach." Rather, it provides a simple index of the amount of time a teacher spends engaged with the curriculum and/or students during instruction. The purpose of collecting this information is to get an understanding of the general amount of time spent on these critical components of the instructional sequence.

To ensure proper data collection during an instructional sequence, it was decided that observations did not begin until teachers offered a verbal or nonverbal (pointing or gesturing) designation of the day's lesson, objective, or content. For example, "Today we will be ... ," "As you recall from our experiment yesterday ... ," "Our learning target for today is ... " are prompts signifying the beginning of the instructional sequence. Upon this cue, the observation began and the teacher was observed teaching within the instructional sequence.

As described previously, time "teaching" is not a quality indicator for the purpose of this discussion but instead an observed behavior during the instructional delivery sequence. "Teaching" provides the student with information, a demonstration, or an example of the content integral to the learning target or daily objective.

With thousands of observations conducted over multiple grade levels and content areas, one would expect differences in the type and scope of specific teacher behaviors within the instructional sequence. In fact, many different types of behaviors were observed during "teaching." For example, students were asked to look at the board and watch while the teacher demonstrated a mathematics problem, or asked to watch a video and listen for an answer to a question, or given an object and asked to make predictions, or simply asked to listen to a description of a definition or activity for the lesson.

Further, some observations involved teachers engaged in demonstration for the entire fifteen-minute observation period while others provided only one to two minutes of review and moved to independent work activities. The following sections present data describing the degree to which the instructional sequence varied across teachers, schools, and students.

Time Teaching—Percentage of Time Observed

During fifteen minutes of instruction, what percentage of time do teachers dedicate to engagement with the curriculum or students? Results gleaned from across all observations indicate that "teaching" was observed during 86 percent of the average observation. While 86 percent may be interpreted as a "B" on a typical grading scale, consider the other 14 percent of the time observed. During 14 percent of the average observation, teachers were not demonstrating, describing, explaining, or providing examples/models—or even looking at students. While not the norm, in some observations, the teachers left the room, were observed to be doing paperwork, or were engaged on a computer.

Time Teaching across Grade Levels

As teaching was observed to occur during 86 percent of the average observation, there is some variation across grade levels. These results are presented in table 3.1. On average, elementary and middle school classroom teachers engage in teaching during 93 percent of observed time. However, the average high-school teacher was observed to be engaged with curriculum and/or students during only 72 percent of the observed time.

This difference is both stark and of concern. It's possible that greater volumes of new information are provided at the younger grade levels, providing a greater need for explanation and demonstration during the instructional sequence. Still, given the level of content difficulty at the high-school level, one would expect that effective instruction would require a clear focus on explanation and demonstration. Of particular concern is the fact that students who are not engaged with the teacher or lesson content are simply less likely to be successful and more likely to eventually be excluded through discipline or drop-out (Reid, Gonzalez, Nordness, Trout, & Epstein, 2004; Snyder, 2001).

Conversations with teachers as they reviewed similar findings provoked potential explanations including insufficient time allocated to paperwork and other duties in addition to teaching. Apparently, teachers often attempt to

Table 3.1   Percentage of Time in Which Teacher was Observed to Be Teaching and Not Teaching—by Grade Level

Grade Level	Teaching (%)	Not Teaching (%)
Elementary	0.93	0.07
Middle school	0.93	0.07
High school	0.72	0.28

find extra time for their additional duties within their classroom instruction. While this is understandable, the amount of time in which students receive no engagement or even supervision from the teacher is predictive of larger failures. Of great concern is the 28 percent of observed time in which high-school teachers are observed to not be teaching.

Observed teaching time varied from a low of 0 percent to a high of 100 percent with the most common result being 100 percent. Thus, the average teacher does use instructional time effectively. Still, a closer look at the data illuminates where some of the variance lies. It is possible that awareness of this variation could lead to positive change in teacher instruction. As the data continue to be described, recall that time "teaching" reflects only one of the multiple pieces of the instructional delivery model—the time the *teacher* is actively engaged.

Teaching across Content Areas

The percentage of time in which the teacher was observed to be teaching within the content areas of reading, math, social studies, and science is presented in table 3.2. Social studies classroom observations revealed the highest percentage of observed teaching, and math classrooms, the lowest percentage. Further, only one percentage point separated the highest observed percentage (social studies) and the second highest (reading) content areas.

Of huge concern is the fact that greater than 10 percent of the observed time in every content area was "not teaching" in terms of the provision of instruction. Although 10 percent of fifteen minutes may seem trivial, this time adds up over class periods resulting in a very different view of the observation findings.

Extrapolating Teaching across Time

When extrapolating the observed time engaged in teaching behavior, small differences in time during a fifteen-minute observation become greater. For example, at the elementary and middle school levels, teaching was observed

Table 3.2   Percentage of Time in Which Teacher was Observed to Be Teaching and Not Teaching—by Content Area

Content Area	Teaching (%)	Not Teaching (%)
Reading	0.89	0.11
Math	0.85	0.15
Social studies	0.90	0.10
Science	0.87	0.13

Table 3.3 Extrapolating Time Spent Not Teaching across Time (Total Time Students Miss Due to Lack of Instruction)

Grade Level	Time Not Teaching (%)	/Min	/Hour (×60)	/Day (×5)	/Month (×20)	/Year (×9)
Elementary and middle school	7	−4.2 sec	−4.2 min	−21 min	−7 hr	−12.6 days
High school	28	−16.8 sec	−16.8 min	−84 min	−28 hr	−50.4 days

during 93 percent of observed time, leaving 7 percent accounted for as "not teaching." A loss of 7 percent in one minute is only four seconds, but in an hour it is more than four minutes. Within a five-hour day, it is a loss of twenty-one minutes, within a month it is a loss of seven hours, and over the course of a school year, it is a loss of more than sixty-three hours—or 12.6 school days. Clearly, this is not an exact loss of time, but it demonstrates the great impact of a few seconds over a time span.

This collection of thousands of fifteen-minute classroom observations provided a lens by which to glimpse into instruction delivery. Findings from this collection revealed a cause for concern when considering the impact of seemingly insignificant amounts of time over a school year.

TEACHER-PROVIDED DIRECTIONS TO STUDENTS

Recall that the direct and explicit instruction model includes review, engaging presentation of content material, guided practice, feedback, and independent practice (Roshenshine & Stevens, 1986). The data on teacher-provided directions is an index of the frequency with which the teacher provides a directive or command to a student—with the assumption that the student is to follow the command or be deemed noncompliant. A direction is distinct from the opportunity to respond (OTR) which is discussed in chapter 4. A direction is a command that is not directly related to the curriculum. For example, "Get out your textbook, please, and turn to page 43," is a direction. In contrast, "Who can describe the water cycle from the diagram on page 43?" is an OTR.

Directions are an integral part of an effective lesson. Borich (2011) identified seven indicators of effective lessons, two of which include providing clear directions and the use of "examples, illustrations and demonstrations to explain and clarify" (p. 95). Recall from the beginning of this chapter that Hattie (2009) noted teacher clarity with communication as a top ten contributing factor to student success. At issue here is the degree to which teachers provide directions in the classroom.

Teacher Directions—Rate of Occurrence

Let's begin with a direction. Find table 3.4 below. Yes, this was a simple direction. Directions do not have to be intricate or involve multiple steps for inclusion. Directions were observed within the instructional sequence and recorded using a frequency count. Each time the teacher provided a direction to the target student or group of which the target student was a member, it was counted as an instance. Data from all observations revealed that teachers provide a direction at a rate of 0.28 per minute in the average classroom—or about every 3.57 minutes.

Every four minutes for a direction seems fairly frequent considering a one-hour class period. This would involve the teacher providing about fifteen directives to the students within each period. But these rates vary across grade levels and content areas. Recall our simple direction. Find table 3.4. Read table 3.4. A closer look at the observation data tells us that there are differences in the rate of directions from elementary to middle and high school. In fact, as students move toward the higher school level, the rate of directions decreases reflecting an increase of more than four minutes between directions from elementary to high school.

Teachers frequently inquire as to whether there is a target rate for directions, asking whether they should back down or increase their own rate. There are two critical considerations in answering these questions. The first is whether students are following the directions at the current rate, and the second is whether there are routine directions that could be broken down to create clarity during instructional presentation.

If students are following directions at the current rate with minimal need for repeating and consistent response, then the current rate may be effective and efficient within the instructional sequence. However, if students are not able to follow directions at the current rate, the teacher may consider reducing the number of directions, increasing the clarity of directions, using single-step rather than multistep directions, or combining directions into a classroom routine. For example, the direction to "Prepare your desk for the group work" includes multiple directions. Clarity may be enhanced by breaking this into discrete directions to clear the desk, turn the table toward a peer, and get out one pencil.

Further, the routines under which students work at the high-school level may be more specific with multiple parts, as opposed to the simple step-by-step directions offered at the elementary school level. This may be reflective

Table 3.4 Teacher Rate of Instructional Directions by Grade Level

Grade Level	Rate/Min	Average Minutes between Directions
Elementary	0.38	2:38
Middle school	0.26	3:51
High school	0.14	7:08

Table 3.5 Teacher Rate of Instructional Directions by Content Area

Content Area	Rate per Minute	Average Minutes between Directions
Reading	0.31	3:13
Math	0.29	3:27
Social studies	0.24	4:10
Science	0.18	5:34

of other factors such as the type of task offered, the grade level, and the instructional grouping of students. For example, repetition of directions may be more commonplace at the younger grades as opposed to the upper grades, and independent worksheets may require very little direction compared to a group project.

Teacher Directions by Content Area

Keeping in mind the potential differences in course content, observation data were further analyzed to consider the curricular content area: reading/ language arts, mathematics, science, and social studies. The question asked was whether teacher directions were provided at different rates across content areas such as in a reading class versus a social studies class or a math class versus a science class. Results of this analysis are presented in table 3.5. Overall, the highest rate of teacher directions was observed in reading/ language arts classrooms with an occurrence on average every 3.22 minutes, closely followed by math at once every 3.45 minutes. In contrast, the lowest observed rate of teacher directions was observed during science instruction with an occurrence every 5.55 minutes.

Potential explanations for this finding would require a look into the tasks and methodologies used in the specific content areas and further analysis of interactions across grade level and content area. It is possible that reading instruction at the kindergarten through Grade 3 levels, which typically includes high rates of explicit systematic instruction, would evidence high rates of directions and interaction with the content. In contrast, a high-school physics course may employ an explicit instruction sequence at a differing rate for key concepts while incorporating the skills of reading throughout other content acquisition.

USE OF INSTRUCTIONAL GROUPINGS

Explicit instruction can be provided within the classroom via a range of instructional grouping formats. The formats considered herein as part of the teacher/student classroom observations included whole-group instruction, small-group instruction, one-on-one instruction, and independent work. Each format will be described with an example from classroom observations.

Whole-group instruction was recorded when the teacher provided the instruction to the entire group in the classroom. This grouping varied by number; on the lower end of the spectrum were classrooms with single-digit student numbers and on the higher end were classrooms with thirty or more students. Typically, whole-group instruction involved the teacher standing at the front of the classroom and providing instruction from a slide presentation, marker board, chalkboard, or via other visual aids. Also common in this grouping was teacher provision of explanations or demonstrations to the entire group at the same time.

The specific type of small-group instruction was recorded based on the presence of the teacher. If the teacher was part of the small group, the observation was recorded as "small group with teacher." If the teacher was facilitating (actively supervising) small-group work across the entire class, the observation was recorded as "small group with peers." An example from an elementary classroom included students working in groups of four with a box of math manipulatives to demonstrate math problems—this was recorded as "small group with peers." At the high-school level, a teacher pulled five students to a table to reteach a science experiment protocol prior to the lab work—this was recorded as "small group with teacher."

One-on-one instruction was recorded if the teacher and the target student worked together within the curriculum. Many times this occurred as a reteaching or error correction procedure during independent work assignments. For example, a teacher would locate an error on a student work product during active supervision and stop to provide explicit one-on-one instruction to the student. This was also observed when the teacher-provided instruction with regard to a specific student question to be answered.

Finally, the independent work grouping code was used when students were provided the opportunity to work independently on a task. This might include a reading task, writing, engagement with a worksheet, and engagement with technology or textbooks. The intention of this code captured the time devoted to student work with active teacher supervision but not engagement during instruction and not as purely unsupervised independent practice.

Instructional Grouping—Percentage of Time Observed

Across all observations, whole-group instruction was observed most often, averaging 56 percent of observed time. Independent work was observed 26 percent of the time, small-group instruction with teacher 9 percent of the observed time, small-group instruction with peers 8 percent of the observed time, and one-on-one interaction between the teacher and student 2 percent

Table 3.6   Percentage of Observed Time in Instructional Groupings

Grade Level	Whole Group	Small- Group Teacher	Small- Group Peers	One-on- One	Independent Work
Percentage of observed time	56	9	8	2	26

Table 3.7   Instructional Grouping by Grade Level

Grade Level	Whole Group (%)	Small- Group Teacher (%)	Small- Group Peers (%)	One-on- One (%)	Independent Work (%)
Elementary	59	26	8	2	30
Middle school	62	3	8	1	26
High school	51	8	8	2	32

of the observed time. In fact, just the combination of whole-group and independent student work was observed 82 percent of the observed time. These data are presented in table 3.6.

Instructional Grouping by Grade Level

Some variations in how teachers use instructional groupings are apparent across grade levels. However, at all three grade levels, whole-group instruction continues to be the most frequently observed type of grouping used by teachers, with independent work the second most frequent. Interestingly, at the elementary level, small-group instruction with the teacher is a close runner-up for the second place with 26 percent of observed time—just behind independent work at 30 percent.

In middle school, small-group instruction with peers was observed more frequently than small-group instruction with the teacher. In contrast, high-school classrooms tended toward a small-group instruction with the teacher than did middle school classrooms. Yet, one-on-one instruction with the teacher remained fairly consistent across grade levels. This most intensive and individualized instruction was observed only between 1 and 2 percent of the total observed time across all grade-level classrooms. The time spent in instructional groupings by grade level is presented in table 3.7.

Instructional Groupings by Grade Level and Content Area

To fully examine the multiple categories within the instructional grouping variable, instructional grouping by grade level was broken out by

Table 3.8   Instructional Grouping by Content Area—Elementary School

Content Area	Whole Group (%)	Small-Group Teacher (%)	Small-Group Peers (%)	One-on-One (%)	Independent Work (%)
Reading	59	10	6	2	23
Math	64	5	8	2	20
Social studies	60	3	16	2	19
Science	73	2	10	1	14

Table 3.9   Instructional Grouping by Content Area—Middle School

Content Area	Whole Group (%)	Small-Group Teacher (%)	Small-Group Peers (%)	One-on-One (%)	Independent Work (%)
Reading	61	2	8	1	29
Math	65	1	6	1	27
Social studies	65	2	10	0	23
Science	65	0	11	1	22

content area. Table 3.8 includes the percentage of time each instructional grouping was observed by content area in elementary school classrooms. This analysis provides a more discrete lens into grade levels and further assists us in describing potential, unique instructional characteristics in the content areas.

Across all elementary classroom observations, small-group instruction with the teacher was recorded 26 percent of the observed time. But while observing during science content, this grouping was seen only 2 percent of the observed time. In contrast, while whole-group instruction across all elementary observations was recorded 59 percent of the observed time, 73 percent of science lessons in the elementary were observed to occur in the context of the whole group. At face value this is somewhat counterintuitive as one might expect science content to be more lab-based and conducted in small groups. Explanations for the resulting differences are not readily apparent from the data.

The middle school observations followed a profile similar to the overall observation findings for instructional grouping with whole-group instruction observed most often and independent work following in frequency. Further, at the middle school level there is little variation across content areas, indicating that teachers at this level are less likely to change groupings based on content. Findings from the middle school observations are presented in table 3.9.

Table 3.10 Instructional Grouping by Content Area—High School

Content Area	Whole Group (%)	Small-Group Teacher (%)	Small-Group Peers (%)	One-on-One (%)	Independent Work (%)
Reading	61	1	5	1	32
Math	54	2	12	2	31
Social studies	54	2	14	1	29
Science	64	0	6	0	29

Table 3.10 presents instructional grouping observations from the high-school classroom observations by content area. Again at the high-school level, whole-group instruction occurs most frequently with independent work following in frequency across all content areas. Similar to middle school but distinct from elementary, high-school teachers do not appear to change instructional groupings based on academic content areas—although they do overall spend more time with students in independent work conditions.

It is important to note that the analyses reported herein represent only the most obvious and theoretically based questions with regard to important variable relationships. The sheer number of variables and observations present in the database is such that addressing every possible angle is beyond the scope of this text. Ultimately, there are many additional questions to be asked and answered regarding the dynamics of an array of variable relationships. For example, how does instructional grouping impact a teacher's use of opportunities to respond and provision of feedback? Does one particular instructional grouping increase the likelihood that students are on task or disruptive during independent work or whole-group instruction? Moreover, to this point, none of these analyses has examined more demographic variables related to schools, teachers, or students.

IMPLICATIONS FOR TEACHERS

As described earlier in this chapter, teaching involves the demonstration or description of a term, concept, procedure, or topic in such a manner so as to increase the probability of student mastery—and success. Effective instruction further promotes student success, encouraging time engaged with the curriculum, and providing ample structure and guidance to address varied skill levels (Ellis & Worthington, 1994). In essence, explicit instruction provides the highest empirical probability for promoting success for the learner.

Any focus on teaching must account for the teacher's engagement with the curriculum as well as the discrete behaviors involved in the instructional sequence. Directions were observed more frequently at the elementary level and less frequently at the high-school level. As was briefly discussed, the question of importance from this discussion is in how this information might help a teacher plan for maximum clarity within a lesson. While this is not a typical consideration for lesson planning, perhaps it would benefit teachers to more carefully plan for how directions will be broken down and delivered as part of a plan.

Finally, as a component of the instructional sequence, the instructional grouping during teaching was observed and described by grade level and within content areas at separate grade levels. A general profile emerged with whole-group instruction and independent work as the prominent instructional groupings observed across grade levels. It is frequently expressed that high-school settings maintain the reputation of whole–group, lecture-type instruction. However, the observations collected here noted whole-group instruction as the primary mode of instructional delivery in all grade levels and content areas.

Recall that explicit instruction involves an instructional sequence that includes review, engaging presentation of content material, guided practice, feedback, and independent practice (Roshenshine & Stevens, 1986). In this chapter, presentation of content material—teaching, guided practice—providing directions, and instructional grouping during presentation are described based on classroom observations. While these three areas are not all-encompassing teacher behaviors within the explicit instruction model, they do provide a foundation for additional areas of effective teacher behavior including the use of feedback and OTRs. These areas are discussed in detail in the following chapters.

Chapter Four

Engagement

Teacher and Student Interaction as a Predictor for Success

Tell me and I forget. Teach me and I remember. Involve me and I learn.

—Benjamin Franklin

GUIDING QUESTIONS

Teachers

1. Why might the concept of "student engagement" begin with the teacher?
2. Considering the content and grade level in which you have the most interest, what might be some of the best strategies for increasing student engagement?

Administrators

1. What characteristics would you expect to see in an effective schoolwide system designed to increase the number of opportunities to respond across content and grade levels?
2. What changes might you encourage teachers to make to a typical lesson plan template in order to increase the likelihood of observing more opportunities to respond?
3. Math and reading teachers tend to provide students more opportunities to respond than other content-area teachers. What characteristics of math and reading lesson plans might lead to this disparity, and how might you go about relaying this information in a positive way to content-area teachers?

While the teacher's knowledge of, and ability to actively engage in, the curriculum is a critical component of effective instruction, the ability of the teacher to actively engage students in the lesson at hand is arguably even more critical to the eventual success of students. It would be difficult to find an educator, or anyone for that matter, who would argue that having students spend less time attending to tasks or teacher instruction is beneficial for their academic or social-behavioral outcomes. Clearly, educators want students to be highly engaged in all aspects of the instructional experience.

Engagement refers to the appropriate ways that students can participate and interact during classroom instruction (Greenwood, Horton, & Utley, 2002; Simonsen, Fairbanks, Briesch, Myers, & Sugai, 2008). Engagement is considered a critical component in order for learning to occur. While it is often viewed in terms of helping students to achieve academic success, students who are engaged in the instructional process also are less likely to exhibit inappropriate behaviors (Conroy, Sutherland, Snyder, & Marsh, 2008; Simonsen, Fairbanks, Briesch, Myers, & Sugai, 2008; Sutherland & Wehby, 2001).

As teachers prepare their daily lessons across a variety of content or topical areas, they certainly hope their instruction will be engaging to the point that students will be active participants throughout the instructional sequence. However, hoping that students will be engaged is not enough. It is not reasonable to expect a student to master content on his or her own without formal instruction. Content instruction is a teacher-driven process that requires specific pedagogical procedures be in place to increase the probability that students will master the content.

In the same vein as pedagogical procedures designed to promote content mastery, if teachers want students to be engaged in the lesson, they must plan for it and build specific practices into their teaching. A student's level of engagement is completely dependent upon the teacher's ability to promote engagement through the use of systematic practices geared toward making the student an active, or in some cases a passive, participant in the lesson. As stated previously, one of the key predictors of student success is the degree to which the student is engaged in instructional content (Berliner, 1990; Kidron & Lindsay, 2014).

Given the importance of student engagement, this chapter provides an overview of the degree to which teachers are using procedures that promote student engagement across a variety of conditions. Engagement is discussed within the context of grade level, content area, and types of instructional delivery methods. Additionally, the relative amounts of engagement types (active, passive, and off task) across grade levels and content areas will be discussed, along with a look at the degree to which teachers appropriately respond to students' raised hands across grade levels and content areas.

INCREASING ENGAGEMENT

If the goal is to get teachers to increase the level of student engagement in their classrooms, there should be a clear rationale for why this is an important endeavor. In short, student engagement in instruction is correlated with student achievement (Conroy et al., 2008). The more students are engaged with teacher-driven instruction, the greater the probability that students will demonstrate higher levels of achievement. While some responsibility for being engaged may fall to the student, during instruction, teachers hold the primary ability to manipulate levels of engagement through their own instructional behavior.

Consider a student who is sitting at his desk drawing pictures during a math lesson. The teacher could simply ignore and let the student continue to be off task while the teacher continues with the lesson. Or, knowing that the student is not going to learn the content of the lesson and therefore be less likely to be able to complete the independent practice successfully, the teacher can choose to take steps to engage the student in the lesson. In fact, one would expect professional teachers to do everything in their power to increase the probability of success for their students.

Just as we would not sit back and expect students to figure out how to multiply fractions without specific instruction on how to do so, it is counter-productive to expect students to figure out how to engage during instruction on their own without specific actions on the part of the teacher to increase the ability of students to do so. If increased engagement is equated to an increased probability for success, we have a justifiable rationale for promoting instruction that leads to increased engagement, and teachers should incorporate practices that do so into their instructional practices.

The intention of increasing engagement is to create a relationship in the student and teacher dyad that provides the student with greater chances for successfully mastering various instructional areas. Also it creates a systematic way for the teacher to manipulate engagement levels to promote improved outcomes for the student. As such, taking steps to increase student engagement should not be seen as an added burden in the teaching process that will eat up both planning and instructional time. Instead, it should be viewed as a component of effective instruction that, with time, will become a natural part of the teaching process.

When considering the conditions under which teachers should implement instructional practices that have the power to increase engagement, the answer is relatively simple. An increase in engagement has the power to improve achievement in a variety of areas. As such, practices that promote engagement should be used whenever the desired outcome is an increase in student knowledge or performance. This can involve instruction in academic content or skill areas or instruction in social behavioral skills.

How to Increase Engagement

Working from a definition of engagement as being the ability of students to appropriately participate and interact with instruction, it would be easy to assume that a variety of actions could be employed by teachers to promote increased engagement for students. However, the primary strategy used by teachers to increase engagement in educational settings is the provision of opportunities to respond. An opportunity to respond occurs when the teacher provides the student with an opportunity to actively respond within the curriculum in some way by presenting students with requests, questions, or directions (Sutherland, Alder, & Gunter, 2003).

Opportunities to respond can take several forms but the goal is always to provide a variety of opportunities for student response, thereby increasing levels of engagement. This can be achieved by providing questions (e.g., close-ended, open-ended, recollection of facts) and directives that create specific tasks for students to complete (e.g., Please write the answer to the math question on the board.). Teachers can also vary the types of questions being asked so that students are asked questions along a continuum of difficulty, with some questions requiring higher level thinking in order to respond.

When considering opportunities to respond, teachers may provide two major categories—group and individual. As one might guess, individual opportunities are those that require a response from an individual student. A group OTR, on the other hand, occurs when the teacher poses a question or prompt to the entire group and all students have the opportunity to respond in unison. This is sometimes called choral responding. In addition to opportunities being presented in individual and group format, responses from students can come in the form of verbal or gestural (e.g., hand-raising, colored paddle raising, discussion with peer, building example) responses.

Teachers can get very creative in finding ways to provide opportunities to respond for their students, and essentially all opportunities to respond fit within the typical teacher/student instructional sequence. However, it is important that teachers align the types of, and levels of, difficulty with student abilities. Further, it is critical that students are able to respond correctly to a minimum of 80 percent of opportunities given. Success rates below 80 percent will be insufficient to predict future success and independence and may also provoke students' task avoidance behaviors as a means of avoiding failure.

Providing opportunities to respond is the primary tool for increasing levels of student engagement during instruction. This is particularly important for students who are struggling with academic and/or social behavior. The more they are engaged, the greater the opportunity for increased achievement, both academically and socially. Teachers can start by focusing on students who attend the least in class and providing them with increased opportunities, both individually and in a group format. Teachers can also focus on the class as a whole, primarily through group opportunities. Increased opportunities to respond benefit all students.

OBSERVATIONS: WHAT TEACHERS TYPICALLY DO TO INCREASE ENGAGEMENT

As discussed previously, providing opportunities to respond is a natural way for teachers to increase student engagement. It fits into the typical instructional model and can be implemented with relative ease. Given this, it would be normal to make the assumption that all teachers provide students with opportunities to respond. After all, isn't that what teachers do? Ask students to answer questions or complete tasks? Of course, that is part of just about any instructional observation anyone would see. However, it is not enough to simply provide opportunities to respond. The number or rate of opportunities is critically important.

While target rates of opportunities per minute may vary slightly in the literature, a safe target rate for teachers to provide students during instruction is three per minute (Haydon et al., 2010). Research has shown that students are significantly more likely to be actively engaged when rates of OTR are at this minimum level. Again, this assumes that the student is able to respond correctly to at least 80 percent of the opportunities given. A gradual increase in the rate of opportunities given is ideal. It is necessary for teachers to monitor and preferably graph the number of opportunities given during both instruction and independent practice.

So, given that we know the importance of increasing student engagement by providing a sufficient number of opportunities to respond, what does the provision of opportunities to respond really look like in the classroom? How are teachers engaging students in their instruction? To be sure, during our observations, teachers did provide opportunities to respond to students, just as you might assume. Questions were asked and directives and instructions were given that required responses from students. The more important question really is, were opportunities to respond being given at desired rates?

It is safe to say that teachers provide students with opportunities to respond in essentially any instructional interaction. However, as stated previously, the critical variable in the provision of opportunities to respond is the rate at which teachers provide these opportunities. Just because it is a natural part of both formally and informally assessing a student's grasp of the content, providing opportunities to respond in an effective manner is not necessarily part of a teacher's repertoire.

Let's assume that we are aiming for the target rate of three per minute. If providing fewer than this recommended rate is predictive of decreased levels of engagement in classrooms, several questions become very important when considering the current state of teaching practices relative to opportunities to respond in our classrooms.

How many opportunities to respond are teachers giving in classrooms? Does it vary by type of opportunity to respond? By grade level? What about different content areas? Do some areas naturally provide more opportunities to respond? What about instructional delivery method? Do certain types of instructional delivery methods provide greater numbers of opportunities to respond? And how does this correlate with engagement levels? Does a higher rate of opportunities to respond actually result in increased student engagement in the classroom?

The following is a discussion of findings that will provide a clearer picture of what is happening in the classroom relative to these questions. And, hopefully this will signal an alarm regarding the need to adjust practices to more closely align what is actually happening in the classroom with what research tells us should be happening. As you will see, the data indicate a discrepancy between what should be happening to promote student engagement and what is actually happening in classrooms.

Opportunities to Respond across Grade Levels

Most people have an image in their minds of what instruction looks like in classrooms of varying age groups. You might envision elementary rooms as having a more smaller group, highly interactive instruction, while middle and high schools move to more of a lecture format of instruction. It is difficult to generalize all elementary or secondary classrooms into one specific description. To be sure, all classrooms have variables that can make them more or less engaging for students. Different content areas and instructional delivery methods certainly have the potential to impact the level of engagement in classrooms.

Considering the effectiveness of providing opportunities to respond in increasing engagement, it is easier and more accurate to use this as a metric for reviewing engagement across different grade levels. Regardless of student age, engagement with the teacher's instruction and the content at hand is critical for student success. Table 4.1 presents observation data on teacher-provided opportunities to respond across grade levels. In reviewing the data, a troubling trend emerges for students as they progress through their schooling.

The obvious big picture that emerges is that students receive fewer than the recommended number of opportunities to respond at all grade levels. Even more, they receive progressively fewer opportunities as they move through

Table 4.1 Teacher-Provided Opportunities to Respond per Minute and (Average Number of Minutes between OTRs) across Grade Levels

Grade Level	Group OTR	Individual OTR	Total OTR
Elementary	0.82	0.15	0.97
	(1:13)	(6:40)	(1:02)
Middle school	0.62	0.07	0.69
	(1:37)	(14:17)	(1:27)
High school	0.48	0.05	0.53
	(2:05)	(20:00)	(1:53)

the grade levels. Elementary students receive 0.97 opportunities to respond per minute. That is less than one opportunity per minute—far fewer than the research-based three opportunities per minute that are desirable during instruction. The number only decreases from there. Middle school students receive 0.69 total opportunities to respond per minute while high-school students receive 0.53 per minute.

When breaking down the types of opportunities being provided, the data indicate a strong preference for group opportunities to respond versus individual opportunities at all levels. At the elementary level, individual opportunities were provided at a rate of 0.15 per minute, followed by 0.07 at the middle school level, and 0.05 at the high-school level. In that same vein, group opportunities to respond progressively decreased as students moved to secondary classrooms with 0.82 opportunities per minute being provided at the elementary level, 0.62 per minute for middle school students, and 0.48 per minute for high-school students.

It is also interesting to note in table 4.1 the average amount of time between opportunities to respond. A similar trend emerges with students waiting for longer periods of time for opportunities to be presented. There are minor differences in the time between total opportunities (range of 1:02 to 1:53) but drastic differences in wait time between the presentation of individual opportunities to respond (range 6:40 at the elementary level to 20:00 at the high-school level).

A few things become very clear from the observation data. The provision of opportunities to respond is occurring at alarmingly low rates for students at all grade levels. While higher rates are being provided at the elementary level, even those rates are falling far below recommended rates. There is much room for improvement in this area. While lower rates may be inherent at secondary levels due to variability in instructional delivery practices, an increase in the rates also have the potential of improving student engagement, and thus, achievement levels. Providing opportunities to respond is completely in the hands of the teacher.

Opportunities to Respond across Content Areas

While not as drastic as the differences in the provision of opportunities to respond across grade levels, differences in the rate of providing opportunities to respond also exist across content areas. Both reading and math content teachers provide higher rates of opportunities to respond than both social studies and science content teachers. In addition, reading and math content teachers had less average time between providing opportunities to respond. Observation data on opportunities to respond across content areas are presented in table 4.2.

Both reading and math content teachers provided similar rates of total opportunities to respond (reading = 0.79 per minute, math = 0.84 per minute), with social studies (0.69 per minute) and science (0.60 per minute) lagging behind. Interestingly, both reading and math teachers provided exactly the same (i.e., 0.10) individual opportunities to respond with an average of ten minutes between individual opportunities, while science teachers doubled that wait time between individual opportunities with an average of twenty minutes between individual opportunities. There were relatively minor differences in the provision of group opportunities to respond across content areas.

The key thing to remember when reviewing the data is that they were collected during the heart of instructional time. Still, the rates all fall short of recommended practice. While the rates for math and reading may be higher due to inherent differences in the nature of instruction in those content areas, given what is known about the positive effects of providing higher rates of opportunities to respond, there is a clear need to improve these rates across all content areas. This brings to light a concern in how teachers are trained at both the in-service and preservice levels to provide sufficient number of opportunities to respond.

Table 4.2   Teacher-Provided Opportunities to Respond per Minute and (Average Number of Minutes between OTRs) across Content Areas

Content Area	Group OTR	Individual OTR	Total OTR
Reading	0.69	0.10	0.79
	(1:27)	(10:00)	(1:16)
Math	0.74	0.10	0.84
	(1:21)	(10:00)	(1:11)
Social studies	0.62	0.07	0.69
	(1:37)	(14:17)	(1:27)
Science	0.55	0.05	0.60
	(1:49)	(20:00)	(1:40)

CONSIDERING STUDENT ENGAGEMENT

The desired outcome of increasing the number of opportunities to respond is to increase the level at which the student is engaged during instruction. When measuring, student engagement during instruction can be separated into two distinct types: active, when the student has been given a specific question or task and is responding (e.g., the student is asked to read a word written on the board and the student does so), and passive, when no specific question or task has been posed, but the student is attentive and doing what is expected at that time during instruction (e.g., the student is at his seat with his eyes on the teacher during instruction).

While the goal is to have students either actively or passively engaged during instruction, it is probable that there will be times in which they are not specifically engaged. There are two additional possibilities—students could be off task (i.e., not attending to the instruction or responding to direct questions or directives) or there could be downtime in the classroom wherein no requests have been made for the students to be doing anything specific related to instruction. The data reviewed herein helps to create a portrait of the present level of student engagement by both grade level and instructional content area.

Student Engagement by Grade Level

Across all grade levels, students are far more likely to be engaged in some manner than be off task. Further, the percentage of time in which there is no discernable task (i.e., downtime) is relatively low at 3 percent at the elementary and middle level—doubling to 6 percent at the high-school level. This pattern of high school looking different from elementary and middle schools plays out across engagement types. Table 4.3 summarizes data on the levels of active engagement, passive engagement, off task, and downtime across grade levels.

If asked to predict, many would likely guess that elementary students are more actively engaged because of the image many have in their mind of highly active elementary classrooms where students are moving from one activity to another. However, while the differences are minimal, high-school students actually demonstrate a higher level of engagement than both elementary and middle school. In turn, elementary students demonstrate higher levels of passive engagement. But this is likely, at least in part, due to the fact that high-school classrooms make more use of independent work during instruction.

Given the definition of active engagement (doing or working), independent work would logically produce higher rates of active engagement. Similarly, increased independent work would logically produce more off-task behavior, and students in high-school classrooms are off task an average of 12 percent

Table 4.3   **Student Engagement by Grade Level**

Grade Level	Active Engagement	Passive Engagement	Off Task	Downtime
Elementary	0.39	0.55	0.03	0.03
Middle school	0.42	0.50	0.05	0.03
High school	0.43	0.39	0.12	0.06

of instruction as compared to 5 percent for middle school students and 3 percent for elementary school students.

Downtime was identical for elementary and middle school at 3 percent of observed time and only minimally different for high school at 6 percent of observed time. Off-task behavior was observed only 3 percent of the time for elementary students and progressively increased to 12 percent of observed time in high-school settings. When active and passive engagement are combined, elementary students are engaged 94 percent of observed time, middle school students 92 percent, and high-school students drop to 82 percent of observed time. Obviously, the higher the percentage of engagement during instruction, the better the odds are for improved outcomes for students.

Student Engagement by Content Area

Interestingly, student engagement across the areas of reading, math, social studies, and science are remarkably similar. Active engagement ranged from 40 to 41 percent of observed time and passive engagement ranged from 49 to 52 percent of observed time. Off task and downtime also varied little. Additionally, all academic content areas demonstrated active or passive engagement during 89 percent or greater of observed time. Table 4.4 presents data on various forms of student engagement across academic content areas. The consistency with which students exhibit engagement in academic content areas is encouraging. The limited variance may be indicative of a single or limited number of teaching methodologies across the content areas, making use of specific teacher behaviors that promote engagement. While it is always

Table 4.4   **Student Engagement by Content Area**

Content Area	Active Engagement	Passive Engagement	Off Task	Downtime
Reading	0.40	0.52	0.05	0.03
Math	41	0.49	0.06	0.04
Social studies	0.40	0.49	0.07	0.04
Science	0.40	0.49	0.07	0.04

possible to move to higher levels of active engagement, the combined levels of active and passive engagement is definitely promising.

CONSIDERING STUDENT HAND-RAISING AND TEACHER ACKNOWLEDGMENT

When discussing the concept of students being engaged with instruction in the classroom, it is important to remember that the teaching and learning process is dyadic in nature; it is an interactive relationship between the teacher and the student. While the teacher holds the responsibility for creating and maintaining student interest and engagement in the lesson at hand, students have the ability to create opportunities for engagement as well. In general, this is done by the student raising his or her hand to seek teacher attention in class. Students raise their hands for a variety of reasons but the main purpose is to ask a question—which may or may not be relevant to the curriculum. Once a student hand has been raised, the teacher has a decision to make of whether to respond or not to the hand being raised.

How a teacher responds to a student raising his or her hand to ask a question can greatly impact the likelihood the student will attempt to ask a question again in the future. If a student raises a hand for teacher attention and the teacher acknowledges him or her, then the behavior has been reinforced, thus making it more likely that hand-raising will occur again. This in turn may increase student engagement as it provides a predictable manner of attaining attention. If the teacher ignores the raised hand, the student may be less likely in the future to attempt to ask questions, thereby decreasing the level of student and teacher interaction, and potentially the level of active engagement of the student.

Student Questions and Teacher Responses by Grade Level

If asked to predict the rate of students raising hands to ask questions by grade level, most would likely say that elementary students tend to seek more teacher attention in class. Images of several students raising their hands and clamoring for the teacher to select them to respond is common image when thinking of elementary classrooms. In contrast, the image of high-school classrooms where students rarely interact or ask questions may be a prevalent image in many minds. While neither of these images is completely accurate for either setting, the numbers do support these perceptions to some degree. Table 4.5 summarizes the rates of students raising hands and teachers responding.

Table 4.5   Student Hand-Raising Rate per Minute and Teacher Response Rate by Grade Level

Grade Level	Student Questions	Response Rate (%)
Elementary	0.22	40
Middle school	0.14	57
High school	0.11	73

In reviewing data on students raising hands and teachers responding to the hand-raising, a few ideas are prominent. First, as many would predict, students do raise their hands more in elementary school and the amount of hand-raising progressively decreases as students proceed through secondary school. Elementary students raise hands to ask questions 0.22 times per minute, while high-school students raise hands 0.11 times per minute. Middle school students fall in between at 0.14 per minute. This may in part be due to high-school students having more specific and distinct questions to ask related to instructional content.

Elementary students, on the other hand, may be more likely to raise their hands even if they don't have a specific question, as a means to access teacher attention. What is more interesting than the rate of hand-raising is the rate of teachers responding to raised hands. High-school teachers have a much higher response rate to hand-raising by responding to 73 percent of raised hands. In contrast, elementary teachers only respond to 40 percent of raised hands. Again, middle school teachers fall in the middle by responding to 57 percent of raised hands. Given that responding to student queries has the potential of increasing engagement, higher rates of responding is desirable.

Overall, observed rates of teacher response are cause for concern. In virtually all classrooms, hand-raising is taught as an appropriate manner of accessing teacher attention. But even at best, in high school, students are acknowledged only 73 percent of the time when raising a hand. Even a nod from the teacher or a direction to put a hand down would count as a response. If engaging in the appropriate behavior is not an effective means of garnering teacher attention, one would think that students would quickly develop more effective albeit less appropriate forms of disruptive behavior.

Student Questions and Teacher Responses by Content Area

While there are stark differences when looking at the rates of student hand-raising and teacher responding across grade levels, the differences are minimal across academic content areas. Across the content areas of reading, math, social studies, and science, student hand-raising ranges from a rate of 0.14 per minute in social studies to 0.18 per minute in reading and teacher

Table 4.6   Student Hand-Raising Rate per Minute and Teacher Response Rate by Content Areas

Content Area	Student Questions	Response Rate (%)
Reading	0.18	50
Math	0.17	53
Social studies	0.14	57
Science	0.15	53

response rates ranged from 50 percent in reading to 57 percent in social studies. Table 4.6 summarizes this data.

Just as with student engagement by content area, student hand-raising and teacher response rates are remarkably consistent. That is not to say that there is no room for improvement. Across all content areas, teachers are responding to roughly one half of all occurrences of students with raised hands. As with providing opportunities to respond, responding to student hand-raising is a teacher-driven activity. Increasing the response rates across grade levels and academic content areas has the possibility of increasing student engagement.

EXTRAPOLATING ENGAGEMENT VARIABLES ACROSS TIME

In looking at the provision of opportunities to respond in schools, a casual review of the observed rates might not reveal the true depth of the problem. After all, how large of an issue is it if a student is getting one opportunity to respond per minute instead of three? It is important to remember that small differences in hitting the target number of opportunities to respond can become large differences over time. To see a clearer picture of the impact of falling short on the number of opportunities to respond, we can extrapolate the number of opportunities across time. Table 4.7 presents an extrapolation across hours, days, months, and one year.

The information contained in table 4.8 is based on a target of three opportunities to respond per minute, the lowest rate at which there is evidence of a significant effect on student behavior (increased engagement and decreased disruption). Comparing actual to recommended rates provides a good example of how small differences can accumulate to tremendous deficits over time. While elementary teachers demonstrate the highest natural rates of opportunities to respond, students still end up with a deficit of 12,180 opportunities to respond over the course of a month. But even this looks good in comparison to the average monthly deficit of 14,820 opportunities to respond observed in the typical high-school classroom.

Table 4.7 Extrapolating OTRs across Time—Relative to Goal of Three per Minute

Grade Level	Total OTR(Group + Indiv)	/Hour (×60)	/Day(×5)	/Month (×20)	/Year(×9)
Elementary	0.97 (−2.03)	−121.8	−609	−12,180	−109,620
Middle school	0.69 (−2.31)	−138.6	−693	−13,860	−124,740
High school	0.53 (−2.47)	−148.2	−741	−14,820	−133,380

Table 4.8 Extrapolating Unacknowledged Hand-Raises across Time

Grade Level	Hand-Raises per Min	Total Number of Hand-Raises Unacknowledged				
		/Min	/Hour(×60)	/Day(×5)	/Month(×20)	/Year(×9)
Elementary	0.22	0.132	7.9	39.6	790	7,128
Middle school	0.14	0.060	3.6	18	360	3,240
High school	0.11	0.030	1.8	9	180	1,620

In a recent study pulled from this data set, both high- and low-performing, high-poverty high schools were compared by observation outcomes. Schools were matched by size and demographics—all were high poverty and the only difference was that eleven schools received the highest state achievement scores while the other eleven received the lowest. Using a sophisticated hierarchical linear modeling analysis, the only significant difference between the high- and low-achieving schools was the degree to which teachers provided opportunities to respond. Students in high-achieving schools received an average of more than 260 additional OTRs per week (Hirn, Hollo, & Scott, in review).

Another variable related to engagement is the degree to which teachers respond to students' appropriate attempts to access attention. Just as with opportunities to respond, the casual observer may not grasp the significance of a student raising a hand three times during class and only having the teacher respond once. At face value, that may seem inconsequential. However, if we extrapolate the numbers across time, we again start to see the true deficit that is created. Table 4.8 presents an extrapolation of the number of unanswered questions to raised hands across minutes, hours, days, months, and one year. Over time, significant deficits build for students at all grade levels. However, when compared to opportunities to respond, an inverse trend appears. High-school teachers fail to respond to 1,620 hands being raised over the course of a year but this pales in comparison to the 7,128 raised hands left unacknowledged in the average elementary classroom. Again, when only looking at the data in terms of occurrences of students' raised hands and teachers failing to respond, the depth of the problem may not be fully apparent. By extrapolating the data over time, the level of deficits is more striking.

IMPLICATIONS FOR TEACHERS

There is an obvious need to improve both the number of opportunities to respond and the ratio of teachers responding to student hand-raising. Looking at either solely as a rate per minute may not provide an accurate image of the need for improvement. Both of these behaviors are teacher-driven, and thus, changing the number of opportunities to respond or acknowledging raised hands is completely under the control of the teachers who should be building these practices into their normal day-to-day teaching practices.

If we can agree that the goal is to increase active engagement levels on the part of students and that the means to do so is by implementing practices that promote engagement like increasing opportunities to respond and increasing rates of teachers responding to student questions, then the question becomes one of how to best make this happen. That is where the real implications of the findings lie—finding the best way to affect change in instructional practices for teachers. This in turn has implications for teacher educators and for professional development within school systems—an issue that is further discussed in chapter 7.

The idea of promoting opportunities to respond is one that has a distinct possibility of falling through the cracks of teacher preparation programs. While it is becoming more prevalent in special education instructional peda-gogy (MacSuga-Gage & Simonsen, 2015), that is not necessarily the case for all areas of teacher preparation. Therefore, while it may be covered in some teaching methods courses and behavior management courses for some special education teaching majors, it very likely does not appear in teaching methods courses for general education teaching majors. At best, even for special edu-cation teaching majors, its coverage is a hit-and-miss in teacher preparation programs (Oliver & Reschly, 2010).

It is imperative that teacher preparation programs make a concerted effort to include instructional practices like the provision of opportunities to respond as a systematic element of courses that provide instruction in peda-gogical content. Evidence suggests that explicit instruction is more likely to result in teachers delivering target rates of opportunities to respond. Teacher preparation programs should provide in-depth instruction in such practices for all teachers.

While incorporating these practices into teacher preparation programs would be beneficial for preservice teachers, the needs of currently practicing educators must be addressed as well. Systematic professional development geared toward promoting engagement through teacher-driven practices should be implemented by individual school systems. Improving engagement has the potential for improving student outcomes. Only the teacher has the power to implement practices that promote increased engagement. Everything should be done to ensure that teachers have the knowledge and tools to effectively increase student engagement.

Chapter Five

Feedback

Positive and Negative Feedback Ratios as a Predictor for Success

There are two ways of spreading light: to be the candle or the mirror that reflects it.

—Edith Wharton

GUIDING QUESTIONS

Teachers

1. Why is it important for a teacher to provide more positive feedback than negative?
2. In what ways might a teacher "build in" times for feedback over the course of a typical lesson?
3. In what ways could "unnecessary artificial reinforcement" negatively impact student engagement?

Administrators

1. What are some ways you, as an administrator, could ensure that teachers are receiving feedback, especially positive feedback over the course of a typical school day?
2. What suggestions might you offer a teacher who is struggling to provide adequate amounts of feedback to students (especially regarding ways to provide more positive than negative feedback)?

This chapter is focused on the frequency and manner in which teachers provide feedback to students. The term "feedback" simply implies that teachers let students know when they are right and wrong. Clearly, knowing right from wrong or appropriate from inappropriate is crucial in mastering a skill. The student who sees 2 + 2 and solves it at different times as 3, 4, or 5 is really no better off than the student who has no idea of the answer. Thus, feedback is not an add-on, it is an inherent part of instruction. Consider explaining a new skill to some stranger, say shoe tying, but never commenting on whether their practice was right or wrong.

In the field of education at large there is always at least a whisper in the background that providing students with performance feedback is unnecessary, if not downright harmful. Among the most common purveyors of this notion is Alfie Kohn (1999, 2001), who makes a living writing books and providing lectures to parents and schools. His general claim is that praising students (i.e., telling them when they are correct) is manipulative, steals their pleasure, promotes a loss of interest, and reduces achievement. Instead of positive feedback he suggests teachers and parents say nothing, state only what they observed, or simply ask questions—without value judgment.

To support his claims Kohn is adept at relating stories that are emotionally compelling and using the phrase "research shows" to accompany vague descriptions of individual studies (often unreferenced). Unfortunately, humans tend to prefer stories to statistics (Kida, 2006), and a personal tale is more compelling than data. Despite this deflating fact, there is strong scientific evidence showing that feedback is a very powerful strategy for promoting student success (Brophy, 2006; Cameron & Pierce, 2002; Hattie, 2009).

To logically consider the notion that feedback is unnecessary for instruction, let's take the critics of positive feedback at their word. Consider that you are teaching a student that 2 + 2 is equal to 4 and that this is the first time that the student has ever been exposed to this principle. After some basic instruction, you ask the student "what is 2 + 2?" and she answers, "4." What do you do next? Would you give the student a gift—perhaps some candy, toys, or a new pencil? Most would say no to that question, perhaps even recoiling at the thought of providing such tangible consequences.

In reality, most of us would simply tell the student that the answer was correct. You might be enthusiastic, "Wow, that's exactly right—good for you!" or you might be more subdued, "yes, now let's look at the next one." But according to Kohn, your effective instructional choices were to say nothing; to simply note the behavior without judgment, "You just said 4"; or to ask a question without judgment, "Why did you say 4?"—to which assumedly the student answers with the correct reasoning—but you still would not allow to indicate that it is correct.

Now let's look at the flip side of this. Consider the same scenario, but this time the student answers incorrectly, "5." While this is technically an error (and a type of misbehavior), no rational person would argue for a harsh punishment. But what if you said nothing at all; simply noted the behavior without judgment, "You just said 5"; or simply asked a question without judgment, "Why did you say 5?"—to which assumedly the student answers with some reasoning that may or may not be logical—but you are not allowed to pass judgment on that answer. Clearly, under such conditions you have not taught the student right from wrong.

Hattie and Timperley (2007, 81) define feedback as "information provided by an agent (e.g., teacher, peer, book, parent, self/experience) regarding aspects of one's performance or understanding that reduces the discrepancy between what is understood and what is aimed to be understood." Thus, feedback occurs after instruction and provides information to the student with regard to whether or the degree to which their performance was correct. In a review of more than 196 studies, John Hattie (2009) found that the average effect of feedback in classrooms was twice that of average teacher practices, placing it in the top 10 influences on student achievement.

While the debate about the use of feedback will certainly continue and many will find personal stories more compelling than the science, the existing evidence suggests that students have a far greater probability of achievement and continued success when teachers provide frequent feedback. Thus, the remainder of this chapter will focus on the effective use of positive and negative feedback in classrooms.

USING FEEDBACK

The purpose of feedback of any type is to let students know whether their behavior (i.e., demonstration, answer, response) was correct. But why is it necessary that students have this information? Generally speaking, the purpose of providing students with positive feedback after behavior is to make it more likely that they'll do it again. That is, you want the student to understand that a given behavior is correct under one particular circumstance or a set of circumstances—but not under others. In fact, this is the definition of reinforcement: any action taken immediately after a behavior that makes that behavior more likely under those same conditions in the future.

The teacher wants the student to know that $2 + 2$ is equal to 4, but he or she also wants her to know that not every math equation is equal to 4 and that $2 + 2$ is not equal to any other number but 4. Of course, this involves an explicit instructional sequence with modeling and engagement to encourage successful responding, but when students behave, the teacher's feedback is what helps the discrimination between right and wrong, appropriate and inappropriate, or correct and incorrect.

In Hattie and Timperley's (2007) definition of feedback, they refer to it as an action that "reduces the discrepancy between what is understood and what is aimed to be understood." Clearly, if a student already has a skill well in hand and uses it independently, then there is no need for the teacher to provide feedback. For example, adults compute basic addition problems on a daily basis without a need for praise. But when calculating how much cash it will take to buy two items at the check-out counter, you likely do not hear the clerk praise us with "good adding."

Our intention for feedback is to help students learn key skills. As students demonstrate mastery, feedback must fade out. The opponents of feedback are correct about the problems that can be caused by overdoing it. Consider three students who consistently complete their homework without teacher acknowledgment for effort. Then the teacher decides to start heaping praise on the students for effort—and this lasts for a week. When the praise goes away, you might expect student homework completion to subside. The students were already behaving for natural reasons and the teacher sabotaged it with unnecessary artificial reinforcement.

While positive feedback could include provision of tangible items, it could also consist of any action that acknowledges a student's behavior as correct. A nod, wink, pat on the back, thumbs up, or a smile can be just as effectively used to signal the student's success. The goal is to provide feedback that is as minimal and natural as possible so that it can be easily faded with student success. Not all students are alike and some may require highly individualized feedback that may involve more tangible items (e.g., token economy). Still, regardless of where positive feedback begins, the goal is to fade it out completely and allow success to take over.

Negative feedback is technically the same as punishment in that the goal is to get a behavior to decrease. Negative feedback is sometimes referred to as a stop command (e.g., stop doing what you are doing or stop doing it that way). But it can also be delivered in a very mild and instructional manner. Consider that the student answers our basic math problem with an error. You could yell, threaten, or even physically remove the student—but the most effective use of negative feedback is correction. This involves simply leading the student back through the behavior (demonstration, answer, response) with prompts to facilitate success. It is still negative feedback, but the probability of student success in the future is higher when using instruction.

When teaching a new behavior or any skill with which the student is not yet fluent, feedback must occur immediately and with every trial. But as students become more fluent, teacher acknowledgment can be faded—allowing natural success to take over. Most of the personal stories with regard to the problems associated with feedback involve students who clearly have an established ability to perform successfully. But when considering students with a history of academic deficits or disability, even more compelling stories can be used to bolster the overwhelming data in support of feedback as an effective instructional strategy.

OBSERVATIONS: WHAT TEACHERS
TYPICALLY DO TO PROVIDE FEEDBACK

As stated previously, the purpose of feedback is to let students know their behavior (demonstration, answer, response) was correct. This is done by delivering positive feedback. This in turn creates a situation wherein the original behavior is more likely to occur again in the future. Another purpose of feedback is to get a particular behavior (demonstration, answer, response) to discontinue. This is done through negative feedback, and hopefully, corrective feedback.

So, given the importance of delivering feedback, what forms of feedback do teachers actually provide in classroom settings? After 6,752 observations, a few general instructional feedback practices begin to stand out.

First, when conducting large-scale observations of classroom instruction across various grade levels and content areas, it is safe to say that an observer will see all forms of potential feedback being used to varying degrees. The most common feedback observed in classrooms is simple verbal praise for correct responses or actions. Often, teachers respond with a quick "Correct!," "That's right!," or simply saying "Yes" in response to a student supplying the correct response or action following a stimulus presented by the teacher. It stands to reason that this form of feedback would be used most frequently considering its efficiency of use in terms of cost and energy.

Oftentimes, verbal praise for correct responses or actions is accompanied by a gesture (e.g., thumbs up) or some other physical response from the teacher like a smile or a nodding of the head in an affirmative way. Sometimes, teachers use physical motions or gestures in isolation, without any form of verbal praise being provided. While this is a form of reinforcement for most students, teachers should be cautious that their gesture is indicative of a correct response or action from the student to help increase the probability of future correct response or actions.

In terms of negative feedback, the most common form that is observationally evident is a teacher simply saying "No." when a student provides an incorrect response. Sometimes that is followed up with "Try again." or the teacher simply moving to a different student to seek the correct response. When students exhibit a social behavior that the teacher deems inappropriate, the teacher's negative feedback often intensifies and is more direct, telling the student to stop and then follow up with punishment in an effort to stop the behavior from happening in the future.

Perhaps the most disturbing observational trend is the use of negative feedback without corrective follow-up. Consider a student who is asked, "What color is the sky on a sunny day?" When the student responds, "Red," the teacher says "No, that is incorrect," and goes on with the rest of the lesson. If the student and teacher interaction stops at that point, the probability of the student learning the correct response and being able to respond appropriately the next time she is asked is not very good. However, if the teacher takes this opportunity to provide corrective feedback and prompt the student in a way that helps the student to respond correctly, the probability of future correct responding is increased.

When observing instructional interactions, one will see teachers typically using various forms of feedback including positive, negative, and corrective. Just as teachers have different teaching styles, dispositions, and temperaments, the provision of feedback varies across teachers. However, given what is known about the effectiveness of feedback in the instructional process, it is critical to have a clear picture of the levels of reinforcement being provided across different grade levels, content areas, and instructional groupings.

Considering Frequencies and Ratios

A common question with regard to feedback in the classroom is, how much is enough? This is a good question and for the most part the answer is really unclear. However, because observed rates have generally been extremely low (Sutherland, Wehby, & Yoder, 2002), the field likely are in no jeopardy of causing any problems by simply making a blanket statement that everyone should strive to do more. But consider the teacher that provides extremely high rates of feedback, say ten per minute (about seventy times higher than typical). Consider that this feedback is 85 percent negative and only 15 percent positive in nature. Clearly there is more to effective feedback than simple frequency.

Not only is disproportionately negative feedback an indicator that instruction is not working, it also creates a predictor for future student failure. There has been some debate as to the most effective ratio of positive-to-negative feedback necessary to predict sustained student responding and success. A common refrain is that teachers should strive to provide positive feedback at a ratio of 4:1—and this is a good rule of thumb. However, it is clear that higher ratios of positive-to-negative feedback are necessary for students with a deficit, a history of failure, or disabilities. There is a balancing act of sorts in effect here as at some point a strong ratio might negate a low frequency.

But it is not clear where this balance is—and it likely varies from student to student.

For our purposes we'll use the lowest recommended ratio as a baseline for looking at typical teacher practice. As mentioned, four positives to one negative is a commonly referenced ratio. However, the best empirical evidence comes from psychology and suggests that positive mental health functioning can be predicted when persons receive about three positive interactions for every one negative interaction with others (Fredrickson, 1998). Again, while using the lowest recommended ratio may be sufficient for many or even most students, it's also true that there will be a significant number of students who will require more.

Feedback across Grade Levels

If asked to guess, most would probably predict that teachers of younger students would use more positive feedback as these children have many behaviors still being shaped by the teacher. In fact this is what the data do show. However, even at the elementary level, rates of positive feedback are alarmingly low, averaging 0.137 times per minute. This means that a typical elementary student receives some sort of positive teacher feedback during instruction about once every seven minutes and twenty-nine seconds. In middle school, the average student receives positive feedback only once every sixteen minutes and twenty-three seconds and by high school it's only once every half hour. Observation data on feedback across grade levels is presented in table 5.1.

In contrast, most would also guess that teachers of younger students would use less negative feedback (i.e., stop command), but this is only partly true. The average elementary student receives negative feedback from the teacher about once every twenty-six minutes and twenty seconds. However, at the

Table 5.1 Feedback Types as Rates per Minute and Average Number of Minutes between Feedback across Grade Levels

Grade Level	Positive Feedback	Negative Feedback	Correction	Positive to Negative Ratio	Percentage of Errors Corrected
Elementary	0.137	0.038	0.007	3:1	15
	7:29	26:20	142:48		
Middle school	0.061	0.031	0.004	1.74:1	11.4
	16:23	32:15	250:00		
High school	0.033	0.046	0.005	0.65:1	9.8
	30:18	21:44	200:00		

middle school level, negative feedback is less frequent, occurring only once every thirty-two minutes and fifteen seconds on average. Truer to our prediction, by high school, the rate rises dramatically so that the average student receives some sort of negative feedback from the teacher about once every twenty-one minutes and forty-four seconds.

Recall correction is the most effective response to errors or misbehavior. Correction differs from negative feedback in that teachers provide a reteaching procedure involving a set of prompts to facilitate a successful response rather than simply providing a stop command. Despite the evidence for its effect, correction is used infrequently at all levels. The average elementary student making an error can expect the teacher to use correction instead of negative feedback only 15 percent of the time, dropping to 11.4 percent of the time in middle school and only 9.8 percent of the time in high school. Clearly, there is room for much improvement in how teachers respond to failure.

Variations in feedback rates across grade levels make for some interesting variations in ratios of positive-to-negative feedback. To calculate ratios, negative feedback and correction are combined to get a total frequency with which a student receives feedback that an error was made. This sum is then divided by the rate of positive feedback and the resulting quotient becomes the first number in the ratio—positive:negative. Feedback ratios are calculated at 3:0.04 in the typical elementary classroom, 1.74:1 in middle school, and 0.65:1 in high school. Thus, the average high-school student receives more negative than positive feedback during instruction.

While feedback rates vary across grade levels, some big picture ideas emerge from the data. First, feedback rates of every type occur at very low rates. Even at the elementary level where the ratio is 3:1, the rates are so low so as to minimize the effect, especially for students with academic deficits. Second, as students get older there is a general trend toward both less positive feedback and less overall feedback. The ratio of positive-to-negative feedback decreases to the point where high-school students actually receive more positive than negative feedback. Finally, teachers rarely use correction as a response to student errors, even with academic tasks.

Given that feedback has an effect twice that of typical school interventions (Hattie, 2009), its use at such low rates across classrooms is concerning. Considering that the provision of instructional feedback is totally under control of the teacher, questions arise as to the factors that inhibit its use. Perhaps the background whispers about the evils of feedback have had a pervasive effect. But if this were the case, one would expect there to be some variation—and observed rates do not vary greatly across teachers. Moreover, these observations were made only during the fifteen minutes in the heart of instruction—when teachers are driving interaction with students.

Table 5.2   Feedback Types as Rates per Minute and Average Number of Minutes between Feedback across Content Areas

	Positive Feedback	Negative Feedback	Correction	Positive to Negative Ratio	Percentage of Errors Corrected
Reading	0.105	0.037	0.006	2.4:1	8.6
	9:31	27:01	166:40		
Math	0.083	0.033	0.006	2.2:1	15
	12.03	30:18	166:40		
Social studies	0.044	0.038	0.003	1.07:1	7.3
	22:43	26:20	333:20		
Science	0.059	0.039	0.005	1.3:1	11
	16:57	25:38	200:00		

Feedback across Content Areas

Variations in feedback rates are also apparent across academic content areas. In general, reading and math content teachers tend to provide higher rates of positive feedback and slightly lower rates of negative feedback. Across all areas, correction rates are too low to be reasonably compared. Perhaps the most telling data can be found in looking at ratios. Both reading and math teachers have better than two positives for every negative. In contrast, social studies and science teachers provide feedback at ratios just better than even. Observation data on feedback across content areas is presented in table 5.2.

Interestingly, although reading teachers provide the highest level of positive feedback, only 8.6 percent of errors receive correction. In contrast, math teachers saw the fewest student errors and corrected those errors at the highest rate. Overall, social studies teachers provide the least positive feedback and the least correction—showing a ratio of just 1.07:1 and using correction in just 7.3 percent of opportunities. As presented visually in figure 5.1, it is easy to see that while negative feedback rates remain rather constant across content areas, positive feedback is variable.

Once again considering the known effects of feedback in terms of predicting sustained student achievement, such anemic rates across content areas is surprising. Perhaps there is a qualitative difference in how teachers are prepared to teach reading and math as compared to social studies and science—and this accounts for differences in the degree to which feedback is provided. For certain, such low rates prompt concerns with regard to the nature of how teachers are trained to provide content-specific instruction.

Feedback across Instructional Groupings

Instructional grouping variations present another variable that has been considered in terms of the teacher's use of feedback during instruction. Data were

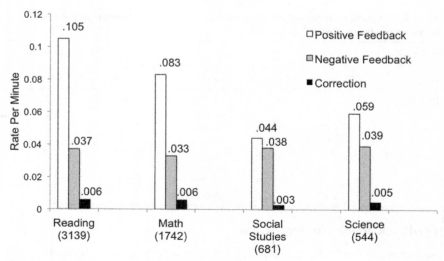

Figure 5.1   Feedback Rates across Content Areas

sorted to find all observations in which 100 percent of the time was spent in whole-group instruction, small-group instruction, or one-on-one teacher and student instruction. Because there were so few observations in which one-on-one instruction occurred for the entire observation, the criterion for inclusion was that at least 90 percent of the observation involved one-on-one instruction. Even this yielded only fourteen total observations but provides a sample for comparison. Table 5.3 summarizes this data.

In general, smaller groupings were associated with higher rates of positive feedback and lower rates of negative feedback. Thus, the ratio of positive-to-negative feedback grows as the grouping gets smaller. In addition, correction

Table 5.3   Feedback Types as Rates per Minute and Average Number of Minutes between Feedback across Instructional Groupings

Instructional Grouping	Positive Feedback	Negative Feedback	Correction	Positive to Negative Ratio	Percentage of Errors Corrected
Whole group	0.087	0.044	0.005	1.77:1	10
	11:29	*22:43*	*200:00*		
Small group	0.168	0.059	0.004	2.6:1	6
	5:57	*16:56*	*250:00*		
1:1 (>90%)*	0.495	0.047	0.016	7.8:1	25.3
	2:01	*2:16*	*62:30*		

*Defined by observations in which at least 90% of the observed time was spent in 1:1 teacher-student instruction.

rates in one-on-one instruction were higher than any other condition, accounting for 25.3 percent of all error feedback. Interestingly, negative feedback rates are actually higher in small group than in whole group. However, much higher rates of positive feedback in small-group settings account for the fact that the ratio is still higher than in the whole-group setting. The ratio in the one-on-one setting is exceptionally high at 7.89:1.

EXTRAPOLATING FEEDBACK RATES ACROSS TIME

It is tempting to look at observed feedback rates and be underwhelmed given that rates are reported per minute. That a teacher might deliver 0.137 versus 0.061 positive feedback statements per minute is difficult to comprehend, and the fact that an entire chapter is spent on this outcome may seem a bit of an overreaction. But remember that per minute differences grow with time. Extrapolation across time reveals that small differences in rates per minute become large differences quite quickly.

Consider the observed ratios of positive feedback to negative feedback and correction in light of the lowest recommended ratio of success to failure at 3:1. Holding negative feedback constant, the degree to which positive feedback rates vary from the 3:1 ratio can be calculated. That is, small variations from the ratio per minute can be observed to grow over time. Table 5.4 presents an extrapolation across hours, days, months, and a year.

Because typical elementary school teachers provide feedback at a ratio greater than 3:1, the typical elementary student receives an increasing surplus of positive feedback across the year. Whether this level is sufficient for students with deficits and a history of failure is unknown, but logic would suggest it is not. At the middle- and high-school levels, poor ratios by the minute add up to alarmingly large deficits. If the goal is for teachers to use for the minimum ratio of 3:1 positive-to-negative teacher feedback, over a year the average middle school student is deficit 67,500 positive feedback instances. That number for the average high-school student is an eye-popping 126,900.

Table 5.4 Positive Feedback Deficit Compared to Lowest Recommended Ratio of 3:1 (Assuming that Negative Feedback is Held Constant)

Grade Level	Ratio	Difference	/Hour (×60)	/Day (×5)	/Month (×20)	/Year (×9)
Elementary	3.04:1	+0.04	+2.4	+12	+240	+2,160
Middle school	1.74:1	−1.26	−75	−375	−7,500	−67,500
High school	0.65:1	−2.35	−141	−705	−14,400	−126,900

One way to increase these ratios would be to decrease the rates of negative feedback and correction. But there are two problems with this line of action. First, rates of negative feedback are already low, averaging only about once every twenty-seven minutes—and correction is all but absent. Second, negative feedback is also a part of instruction. Certainly instruction can be developed to minimize errors and misbehaviors but when they do occur, students need to have that feedback. A more logical approach is to consider strategies for both promoting student success and increasing teacher feedback.

IMPLICATIONS FOR TEACHERS

As has been discussed, feedback is not an addition to instruction. Rather, it is an essential part of teaching. Further, it is well established that effective instruction sets students up to be successful at rates that are higher than failure (errors). In fact, it would be logical to conclude that the larger the ratio of success to failure, the more effective the instruction. Clearly, rising error rates and increasing student failure are signs that instruction is not working. In fact, students from disadvantaged backgrounds, histories of failure, and disabilities will require higher ratios of success in order to be successful.

As a general rule, feedback can be considered simply as acknowledgment— letting the student know whether he or she has been successful. It needn't be tangible, distracting, or overblown in order to be effective. Because some students may enter instruction with low self-confidence in their ability to succeed, even a single failure can at times precipitate a surrender mentality—from a type of learned helplessness. Teachers must strive to find ways to provide quick, clear, simple, and effective feedback to students as part of instruction. However, the more failure a student has experienced, the more intense instruction will need to be to facilitate success, and with more dynamic and obvious positive acknowledgment.

Chapter Six

Mediating Variables

What Teacher and Student Characteristics Make a Difference?

A true teacher defends his students against his own personal influences.

—Amos Bronson Alcott

GUIDING QUESTIONS

Teachers

1. How can I ensure that my students—male and female—are given adequate opportunities to respond?
2. How can I become more culturally responsive?

Administrators

1. How can I support staff to be more culturally responsive?
2. What are some areas for growth to improve culture in my school?

The previous chapters have focused on describing observed rates of rather specific teacher and student behaviors. While some information was presented regarding differences across academic subject areas, there has been little effort to consider how observations may vary across a wider variety of demographic factors. This chapter presents a breakdown of observed rates of teacher and student behavior across a range of other factors—which we refer to as mediating variables. There is no effort here to provide in-depth analysis or to attempt to explain differences, only to report what was observed in as straightforward a manner as possible.

Prior to conducting an observation, the gender and ethnicity of both teacher and student was recorded. Of course, it is possible to cut the data in a number of ways—looking at interaction effects across gender, ethnicity, age, content, and a variety of other variables. But such analyses are beyond the scope of this book. We simply present rates of behavior broken down by gender of both teacher and student, followed by the same types of breakdowns by ethnicity of both teacher and student. The chapter ends with a brief discussion of students with identified challenging behaviors.

GENDER AND INSTRUCTION

Consideration of gender differences in the classroom is well represented in the literature, albeit often with contradictory results. Perhaps some of the variance is, in part, a result of generally low sample sizes and a focus on one or two schools. The results presented here are based on an analysis of the entire data set, covering a full range of schools. Observations were made on every teacher in each observed school and results show that female teachers outnumber males by a ratio of more than 3:1. The following data represents 5,142 female teachers and 1,613 male teachers.

Teacher Gender

Gender differences across teachers has been studied in terms of how they perceive their own efficacy (Schwarzer & Hallum, 2008), job satisfaction (Klassen & Chiu, 2010), and attitudes toward curricular and policy decisions (e.g., Busch, 1995). However, there are no empirical observations of how teacher behaviors differ by gender in the classroom—without regard to student demographics. Table 6.1 presents observed rates of teacher behavior by gender.

Female teachers were generally seen to provide more directions, more opportunities for student responses, and more positive feedback than did their male colleagues. However, rates of negative feedback were equal across male and female teachers. In most cases, differences were substantial, with female teachers providing 58 percent more directions, 77 percent more group opportunities to respond, 58 percent more individual opportunities to respond, and 45 percent more positive feedback.

Table 6.1   Observed Rates of Teacher Instructional Behaviors by Teacher Gender

	Teacher Directions	OTR Group	OTR Individual	Positive Feedback	Negative Feedback
Male teacher	0.18	0.55	0.07	0.05	0.04
Female teacher	0.31	0.71	0.12	0.11	0.04

Table 6.2   Observed Rates of Teacher Duration Variables and Student Behaviors by Teacher Gender

	Time Teaching (%)	Downtime (%)	Whole-Group Instruction (%)	Student Off Task (%)	Student Actively Engaged (%)
Male teacher	78	5	56	9	43
Female teacher	89	4	56	5	41

In addition to the provision of opportunities for students to respond during instruction and the delivery of feedback, observers recorded the percentage of time in which teachers were engaged with teaching and students were engaged during instruction. As introduced in chapter 3, the percentage of time teaching referred to herein is simply a descriptor of the degree to which a teacher is engaged with the curriculum and/or students. Using this definition, female teachers were observed to be engaged in teaching during 89 percent of the average observation, compared to 79 percent for male teachers. Duration variable results by gender are presented in table 6.2.

Part of the difference in teaching is likely attributable to the fact that male teachers are far more likely to be working in high schools, where percentages of time teaching are lower across all subject areas. Downtime was recorded as a duration variable whenever the observer was unable to determine whether there was a teacher expectation—thus impossible to determine whether the student is on task. Overall, downtime was very similar across teacher genders and both female and male teachers were observed to teach to the whole group during 56 percent of observed time.

Interestingly, although students were actively engaged at very similar levels with both female and male teachers, the average student was 80 percent more likely to be observed as off task when under the direction of male teachers. While these are rather low levels overall, 9 percent off task with male teachers and 5 percent with female, a difference of 4 percent every fifteen minutes, is equal to 2.4 minutes per hour during that class. This extrapolates to twelve minutes per week and approximately forty-eight minutes per month during that hour. Thus, the student who is recorded as being off task 4 percent of the time is missing nearly an hour of instruction per month.

Student Gender

Across all observations there were virtually equal numbers of male and female students (50 percent for each). Gender differences across students has been studied in much the same manner as teacher differences, focusing on how they perceive their own efficacy (Pajares & Valiante, 1999), job/school

Table 6.3 Observed Rates of Teacher Instructional Behaviors by Student Gender

	OTR Individual	Positive Feedback	Negative Feedback	Student Disruptions
Male student	0.12	0.09	0.05	0.05
Female student	0.09	0.09	0.03	0.02

satisfaction (Huebner, 1991), and attitudes toward curricular and policy decisions (Jones, Howe, & Rua, 2000). Again, the literature presents mixed results as to whether and how female and male students differ in how they are treated during instruction. Table 6.3 presents observed rates of teacher behavior by student gender.

As has been discussed in chapters 4 and 5, overall rates of teachers' provision of opportunities for student response and feedback during instruction are very low. In some respects these rates are different when considering female versus male students. In terms of having an individual opportunity to respond during instruction, males actually receive about 33 percent more opportunities from the teacher. Further, while female and male students receive nearly identical rates of positive feedback, they are about twice as likely to be disruptive and to receive negative feedback.

The fact that male students receive more negative feedback is not surprising given the elevated rates of disruption. In fact, considering that male students are more likely to be disruptive, one might speculate that teachers engage males more frequently as a means of trying to maintain engagement or bring students back to the lesson. However, as will be discussed at the end of this chapter, following students with challenging behaviors indicates that disruptive behavior is actually a predictor for less teacher-initiated interaction.

In a seminal 1985 review of the literature regarding teacher and student differences related to gender, Jere Brophy concluded that observed differences in the classroom were most likely a result of how the students acted. He suggested that gender roles defined in the dominant culture dictated how students behave and engage during instruction. As was observed herein, although both male and female students are equally likely to be actively engaged during instruction, male students are far more likely to be both off task and disruptive while female students are more likely to be passively engaged. This data is summarized in table 6.4.

Interaction Effects

The most interesting gender questions are those that consider interaction effects between the gender of teachers and students. Table 6.5 presents results

Table 6.4 Percentage Time Observed Off Task and Engaged by Student Gender

	Off Task	*Active Engagement*	*Passive Engagement*
Male student	0.07	0.40	0.48
Female student	0.04	0.42	0.50

Table 6.5 Student and Teacher Behaviors by Student-Teacher Gender Match

Student-Teacher	*OTR Individual*	*Positive Feedback*	*Negative Feedback*	*Disruption*
Male S–male T	0.53	0.05	0.04	0.05
Female S–male T	0.57	0.05	0.03	0.03
Male S–female T	0.68	0.11	0.05	0.05
Female S–female T	0.75	0.10	0.03	0.02

Table 6.6 Student Hand-Raising and Teacher Acknowledgment by Student-Teacher Gender Match

Student-Teacher	*Rate of Students' Hand Raised for Teacher Attention*	*Percentage of Student Hand-Raises Acknowledged by Teacher*
Male S–male T	0.13	0.62
Female S–male T	0.12	0.67
Male S–female T	0.19	0.58
Female S–female T	0.18	0.56

of the interaction between student and teacher gender. In sum, there is very little difference in teacher behaviors across both teacher and student gender and thus no evidence that teacher and student gender matching has any effect on observed teacher practice.

Hand-Raising and Acknowledgment by Gender

A more interesting result regarding gender can be seen in the rates of student hand-raising and percentage of time those hand-raises are acknowledged by the teacher (table 6.6). Both female and male students raise their hand for teacher attention about 30 percent less often with a male teacher. However, in an unexpected twist, male teachers are more likely to acknowledge a raised hand than female teachers—and both female and male teachers are very slightly more likely to acknowledge a student of the opposite gender. Again, this final difference is very small, but it does present some interesting questions regarding student engagement.

ETHNICITY AND INSTRUCTION

Just as with gender, observers designated the ethnicity of both teacher and target student prior to beginning the observation. However, ethnicity is perhaps a bit of a misnomer in that the term "minority" simply refers to any ethnicity other than Caucasian. In reality, we estimate that better than 95 percent of all teachers and students coded as minority are actually African American. We have chosen to use the terms minority and nonminority to designate what is typically thought of as white and nonwhite.

The results presented here are based on an analysis of the entire data set, covering a full range of schools. Observations were made on every teacher in each observed school and results show that nonminority teachers outnumber minorities by a ratio of more than 10:1. The following results are pulled from observations of 6,170 nonminority teachers and 586 minority teachers. Student ethnic makeup across the data set is more evenly distributed with 4,266 nonminority students and 2,491 minority students.

Ethnicity is an important variable when considering the quality of instruction, achievement, and behavior. Minority students are suspended from school at a rate that is more than three times greater than nonminority students (US Department of Education Office of Civil Rights, 2014). Alarmingly, the evidence shows that this disciplinary gap has continually widened over the past forty years (Losen & Skiba, 2010). To be certain, there is a vicious circle of sorts at play as academic and discipline problems are predictors for one another (Rausch & Skiba, 2004; Rocque & Paternoster, 2011).

Potential explanations for these inequities have focused on school integration, income discrepancies, and differential teacher expectations based on student ethnicity. Considering school integration, there is some evidence that the density of black students impacts achievement. While nonminority student achievement does not vary depending on the percentage of minority students in the school, minority students, even when controlling for socioeconomic status (SES), tend to have poorer outcomes in less integrated schools (National Center for Educational Statistics, 2015). There is similar evidence for teacher expectations as research has repeatedly shown that teachers in general have lower expectations for students in low-income schools, where minority are generally overrepresented (Ferguson, 2003; Mickelson, 2001).

Teacher Ethnicity

Table 6.7 presents observed rates of teacher behavior by gender. Overall, there are few differences in how minority and nonminority teachers deliver instruction. What differences are apparent are likely at least in part due to the fact that minority teachers are more likely to be working in low-income

Table 6.7   Observed Rates of Teacher Instructional Behaviors by Teacher Ethnicity

	Teacher Direction	*OTR Group*	*OTR Individual*	*Positive Feedback*	*Negative Feedback*	*Student Disruption*
Nonminority teacher	0.28	0.68	0.11	0.09	0.04	0.04
Minority teacher	0.26	0.63	0.07	0.08	0.05	0.05

Table 6.8   Observed Rates of Teacher Duration Variables and Student Behaviors by Teacher Ethnicity

	Time Teaching (%)	*Downtime (%)*	*Whole-Group Instruction (%)*	*Student Off Task (%)*	*Student Actively Engaged (%)*
Nonminority teacher	87	4	56	6	41
Minority teacher	77	4	59	7	41

schools and dealing with students who present more challenging behaviors during instruction.

In addition to the provision of opportunities for students to respond during instruction and the delivery of feedback, observers recorded the percentage of time in which teachers were engaged with teaching and students were engaged during instruction. The duration variable results by ethnicity are presented in table 6.8.

Considering teacher and student engagement during instruction, nonminority teachers were observed to be engaged in teaching during 87 percent of the average observation, compared to 77 percent for minority teachers—almost exactly mirroring the difference between female and male teachers on the same measure. Otherwise, the degree of downtime, time engaged in whole-group instruction, and student engagement are all equivalent across teacher ethnicity.

Student Ethnicity

Across grade levels and content areas, minority and nonminority students generally receive the same opportunities to respond and positive feedback from teachers. However, minority students are seen to be more than three times more likely to be disruptive and twice as likely to receive negative feedback from teachers. These results are presented in table 6.9.

Unlike student gender, student ethnicity does not predict engagement levels. However, minority students were observed to be two and a half times

Table 6.9   Observed Rates of Teacher Instructional Behaviors by Student Ethnicity

	OTR Individual	Positive Feedback	Negative Feedback	Student Disruption
Nonminority student	0.11	0.09	0.03	0.02
Minority student	0.11	0.09	0.06	0.07

Table 6.10   Percentage Time Observed Off Task and Engaged by Student Ethnicity

	Off Task	Active Engagement	Passive Engagement
Nonminority student	0.04	0.51	0.41
Minority student	0.10	0.50	0.40

more likely to be off task. This difference accumulates to 3.6 minutes per hour, or in the case of a typical one-hour class, these students miss 72 minutes of instruction per month. These results are presented in table 6.10.

Interaction Effects

Consideration of the ethnic match between teachers and students has been discussed for decades (e.g., Adams & Cohen, 1974; Ehrenberg & Brewer, 1995) with very mixed results. According to the US Department of Education's National Center for Education Statistics (2011), only 4 percent of America's teachers identify as non-Hispanic black, while black students make up approximately 15 percent of the population. This is especially the case among black males who make up just over 1 percent of the teacher workforce (Toldson & Lewis, 2012). Differences in student achievement have been reported as being positively related to the availability of teachers who match the students' ethnicity (Dee, 2004; Eddy & Easton-Brooks, 2011; Egalite, Kisida, & Winters, 2015; Winters, Haight, Swain, & Pickering, 2013). However, the reported differences have been relatively small and have not accounted for a range of other potentially important variables (Eddy & Easton-Brooks, 2011; Howsen & Trawick, 2007; Tyson, 2003). As Egalite et al. (2015) have stated, "Whether or not assignment to a teacher of the same race/ethnicity is related to student achievement is an empirical question that has yet to be fully resolved" (p. 45). However, there is much more compelling evidence of how teacher and student ethnicity interact in terms of behaviors and perceptions.

For example, McGrady and Reynolds (2013) found that teachers tend to view students differently based on ethnicity, with Asian students typically viewed more positively and black students less positively by white teachers. Other studies have reported similar findings, citing the most pronounced

Table 6.11   Teacher and Student Behaviors by Teacher-Student Ethnicity Match

Teacher-Student	OTR Individual	Positive Feedback	Negative Feedback	Student Disruption
Teacher minority–student minority	0.07	0.07	0.08	0.06
Teacher minority–student nonminority	0.07	0.09	0.03	0.03
Teacher nonminority–student minority	0.11	0.09	0.06	0.07
Teacher nonminority–student nonminority	0.11	0.09	0.03	0.02

differences among students from low SES (Dee, 2005) and low performers (Egalite et al., 2015). But Takei and Shouse (2008) found that both white and black teachers rated students' work habits differently based solely on ethnicity with black students' work and ability being rated as lower, even after controlling for actual behavior. While the effect was more pronounced for white teachers' ratings, they found that white teachers' perceptions of black students tended to be higher in schools where students were generally of a higher SES.

Table 6.11 presents the results of the interaction between student and teacher ethnicity. In sum, there is very little difference in the degree of opportunities to respond, positive feedback, or negative feedback as a result of teacher and student ethnic matching. Further, while minority students are more likely to be disruptive, this behavior does not appear to be related to teacher ethnicity.

Hand-Raising and Acknowledgment by Ethnicity

Similar to findings with teacher and student gender interaction, there are no clear differences in the rate of hand-raising behaviors across students by ethnicity. However, while nonminority teachers tend to acknowledge hand-raising similarly across student ethnicity, minority teachers acknowledge minority students' hand-raising 10 percent less often than they do for nonminority students. In fact, across all ethnic combinations minority teachers' acknowledgment of minority student hand-raises is clearly the lowest response rate. These results are presented in table 6.12.

STUDENTS WITH DISABILITIES

The regular education classroom continues to be considered a least restrictive environment for students with identified disabilities. In fact, it is the first consideration to be addressed in committee meetings as programs are designed to meet the needs of this diverse group of learners. Because even students with

Table 6.12   Student Hand-Raising and Teacher Acknowledgment by Student-Teacher Ethnicity Match

Teacher-Student	Rate of Students' Hand Raised for Teacher Attention	Percentage of Student Hand-Raises Acknowledged by Teacher (%)
Teacher minority–student minority	0.17	46
Teacher minority–student nonminority	0.16	56
Teacher nonminority–student minority	0.18	51
Teacher nonminority–student nonminority	0.17	53

challenging behavior are increasingly served in the general education classroom we questioned whether this setting provided sufficient rates of effective instructional behaviors.

The interaction between these students and their teachers was considered by looking at observations within the database reflective of a dyad between the classroom teacher and a student identified with challenging behavior. Challenging behavior was defined as a student exhibiting classroom behavior problems that, on at least three occasions, had resulted in a referral to the office. For example, disrupting the class by yelling out, threatening a student, or any physical action toward a student or teacher. These students had been identified prior to observation and were specifically targeted and coded as having behavioral challenges.

Observations of students with challenging behavior ($n = 390$) were compared with a group of students in the same classrooms that were not identified as having challenging behaviors ($n = 437$). Analysis of the observations showed that teachers provided less individual opportunities to respond to curricular questions, increased rates of negative feedback, and a positive/negative feedback ratio of 1 positive to 3.8 negative with students identified as exhibiting challenging behaviors (Hirn & Scott, 2014). Teachers provided similar rates of positive feedback and group opportunities to respond to both groups.

Similarly, differences in student engagement were identified between the two groups. Students with challenging behavior were observed off task more often and exhibiting disruptions nearly three times the rate of those students identified without challenging behaviors (Hirn & Scott, 2014). Observations revealed that students identified as having challenging behaviors exhibited a disruption about every seven minutes, whereas students without such challenges exhibited disruptive behaviors about every twenty-five minutes.

Understanding these observed differences in the interactions between students exhibiting classroom disruptive behavior provides an opportunity for developing instructional plans to address the unique needs of diverse learners in the regular education classrooms.

This collection of observations is a brief but telling picture of the relationship between teachers and students exhibiting behavior challenges. While we would hope to see that these students were the target of more positive attention and receive increased opportunities to be engaged, we found quite the opposite. These results are consistent with the larger literature indicating that students with identified behavioral issues get less and poorer instruction than their typical classmates (Stichter et al., 2009; Sutherland, Lewis-Palmer, Stichter, & Morgan, 2008).

IMPLICATIONS FOR TEACHERS

There is little evidence to suggest that ethnicity and gender are major contributors to observed differences across teachers. Thus, there is little reason to discuss ethnic and gender-matching strategies across teachers and students, despite the fact that such discussions continue in the broader literature (e.g., Dee, 2005; Spilt, Koomen, & Jak, 2012). As Egalite et al. (2015) have suggested, any observed differences are likely due more to the culture within which they occur than to real differences among people of differing ethnicities or gender.

A more practical approach for schools is to have teachers openly discuss and consider how biases might manifest within a given school culture. This would then lead to a concerted schoolwide effort to consider culturally responsive practices as part of what teachers do on a daily basis (Bottiani et al., 2012). While such an approach with considering students with identified behavioral challenges has not been reported in the literature, there is no reason that the same logic of self-reflection, group discussion, and schoolwide goal setting for teachers would not prove equally effective.

Chapter Seven

Implications for the Field of Education

If the children aren't learning, we're not teaching.

—Siegfried Engelmann

GUIDING QUESTIONS

Teachers

1. What support do I need to increase my use of effective teaching practices?
2. How can I increase the opportunities for my students to respond during instruction?

Administrators

1. How can I support my staff to learn and become comfortable implementing effective teaching practices?
2. How can I use the Continuous Professional Growth Model to improve teacher's instruction?

Teaching behaviors can be defined as the manner and frequency of verbal and physical interactions with students during instructional time. Thus, teaching behaviors are the behaviors that teachers use when engaging in effective instruction. As with most important questions, the answer to the question, "What is the ideal instructional practice?" is, "It depends." However, among the long and varied list of available instructional strategies are a set of foundational practices for which there is nearly half a century of empirical support (see Hattie, 2009).

Evidence supports the use of such basic teacher behaviors as modeling, clearly stated directions, prompts and reminders, and the provision of opportunities for students to respond to during instruction. These teacher practices occur in the context of instructional delivery and can be observed and measured in terms of frequency or rate of occurrence. Another teacher strategy, feedback for both desired and undesired responses, is perhaps as simple and as important as any that a teacher can provide during instruction.

To consider the field of education at large without considering the degree to which the most effective practices are implemented is a fool's errand.

THE IMPORTANCE OF PEDAGOGY

While for any particular strategy it is likely that someone can recall a particular student for whom the strategy was ineffective, these foundations still present a best chance scenario when considering strategies for the primary tier (see Hattie, 2009). When students fail, the first thought should be with the quality of instruction and, although less evidence-based strategies might be considered, this consideration is done only after insuring that effective strategies have actually been implemented with fidelity. But too often the term "innovation" is tossed out as a standard response to student failure, and there are a couple of important points worth considering.

First, innovation must be more than just arbitrary novelty. There is nothing really innovative about "different" if that method has been demonstrated to be less effective. For example, consider that roofs leaking all over town and shingles do not seem to be working when reinstalled. It would be innovative to use thatched straw. But what if shingles weren't being installed correctly? Wouldn't it make more sense to install the shingles correctly than to use thatch—a method we know from previous evidence is not effective?

A basic review of the educational literature in any content area reveals that innovation easily trumps evidence-based practice in terms of popularity. Furthermore, evidence-based practices are very often the target of derision in the educational literature—made the scapegoat for poor student achievement. But the data presented herein beg the question as to whether our educational shingles were ever installed correctly in the first place. It is illogical to assume that a practice will be effective or a strategy will be successful if it is never implemented in a manner consistent with what research has demonstrated.

Second, we know what good instruction looks like and, as has been reported herein, teachers use these practices at exceptionally low rates, if at all. In fact, because effective practices are implemented at such consistently low rates, we really don't know what "optimum" levels are. For example, across all observations teachers were observed to provide positive feedback at a mean rate of

.1 times per minute—with a range of 0 to 2.1 and a standard deviation of .1. Because significantly higher rates have not been observed in naturalistic settings, we really don't know what effects might be possible. However, it is possible to consider a hypothetical relationship between teacher and student behavior. Figure 7.1 provides a graphic depiction of this hypothetical relationship.

It is logical to assume that the relationship between teacher behavior and student success is not purely linear—but more likely S-shaped. At the bottom end of teacher behavior the difference between rates that are all very close to zero is unlikely to make much difference. At the top end, there is likely a point of diminishing returns, where increasing feedback from one hundred times per minute to one hundred and fifty times per minute is unlikely to make much difference—or may even produce a deleterious effect. For any given strategy, the key is to find the level of teacher behavior that is associated with the highest level of student success. This represents the optimum level for practice.

In reality, optimum levels of teacher behavior probably vary depending on a number of factors including student age, content area, and prior learning history—or a history of success. The problem with the existing data is that naturalistic observations are all toward the bottom end of possible teacher rates. Thus, it is impossible to know whether optimal rates have been observed. However, because observed rates of these evidence-based practices have been so consistently low, it is logical to assume that an optimal rate is higher than what has been observed.

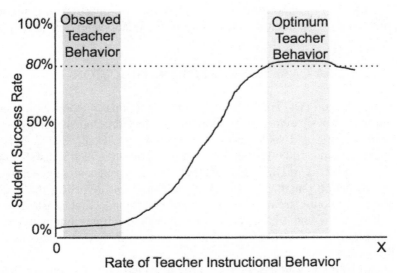

Figure 7.1 Observations of Teacher Behavior Rates and the Hypothesized Scope of All Possible Rates

The Impact of Effective Teachers

Other than parents, teachers play perhaps the largest role in predicting the lifetime success of students (Pianta, Belsky, Vandergrift, Houts, & Morrison, 2008). Most immediate of these impacts is academic achievement as high-performing teachers have been shown to increase reading by an effect size of better than .3 and math by an effect size of .5 (Nye, Konstantopoulos, & Hedges, 2004; Stronge, 2013). A highly effective first-grade teacher can have a significant impact on students' achievement scores through the sixth grade (Konstantopoulos & Chung, 2011).

Students receiving effective academic instruction are also less likely to exhibit problem behavior (Rivkin, Hanushek, & Kain, 2005) and more likely to experience academic success (McIntosh, Chard, Boland, & Horner, 2006). Alarmingly, evidence suggests that teachers in high-need schools engage in fewer rather than more effective instructional strategies (Stichter et al., 2009). In general, the probability of student success with a given curriculum can be maximized by instructional practices that increase the degree to which students are engaged with instructional content (Brophy, 2006). That is, effective instruction is, at least in part, a set of practices that the teacher uses to engage students.

We know that, without fail, the teacher's behavior plays a major role in predicting the success of the students they teach. Logically, the teacher must take on the responsibility for providing the instruction necessary to ensure student success. Further, when instruction is not successful, it is the teacher who must change first. Robert Pianta (1996) states this most succinctly, "The asymmetry in child–adult relationship systems places a disproportionate amount of responsibility on the adult for the quality of the relationship" (p. 73).

A CASE FOR DIRECT INSTRUCTION

Direct Instruction (DI) is an oft-maligned instructional method with a large and strong body of evidence in support of effect on student achievement, problem solving, and self-esteem (Cooper, Hirn, & Scott, 2015; Gersten, Darch, & Gleason, 1988; Hattie, 2013). It is important to distinguish between the specific practice of Direct Instruction (capital DI) and a more general term direct instruction (small di) that refers to instruction involving the teacher directing instruction from the front of the classroom. Direct Instruction is explicit but the lesson is based on teacher-selected examples, interactive modeling, high rates of student responding, provision of immediate and consistent feedback, and guided practice to mastery.

As part of a study to assess the degree to which effective teacher behaviors are associated with DI, a series of observations were conducted with teachers and teachers in training using *Reading Mastery* with a small group of elementary students who had been identified as having chronic reading deficits over multiple years. These observations were not included in the database that has been described herein because they were not naturalistic. That is, these teachers were specifically trained in DI and were scheduled for observation during a DI lesson.

This effort resulted in four elementary DI reading observations which were compared to 16 elementary small-group reading instruction observations and 515 elementary whole-group reading instruction observations. While the small number of DI observations precludes a more systematic analysis, simple descriptive comparisons are often quite profound in terms of differences in teacher and student behaviors.

In terms of the amount of instructional time in which teachers are engaged with either curriculum or students, teachers in the DI condition were teaching during 100 percent of observed time. This is not surprising as the nature of DI is such that the teacher leads instruction throughout the lesson. Similarly, teachers in the DI and typical small-group conditions provided more directions to students than what was observed during whole-group instruction. These comparisons are represented graphically in figure 7.2.

Students in the DI condition were far more likely to be actively engaged, averaging 91 percent across observations. Interestingly, even the typical small-group reading condition saw averages of only 38 percent active student engagement, slightly less than the 41 percent active engagement observed in whole-group reading. This is surprising as it seems logical that a smaller teacher-student ratio would allow teachers to engage students in a more hands-on manner. In contrast, students were far more likely to be disruptive in whole-group settings. No disruptions were observed in the DI condition, but again the small number of observations is an obvious limitation. These results are summarized in figures 7.3 and 7.4.

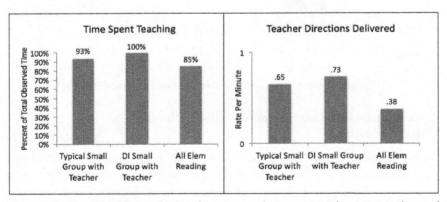

Figure 7.2   Time Teaching and Directions Comparisons across Direct Instruction and Typical Reading Instruction

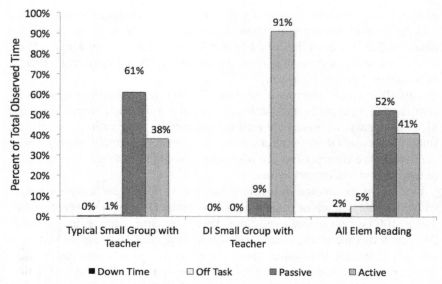

Figure 7.3   Student Engagement across Direct Instruction and Typical Reading Instruction

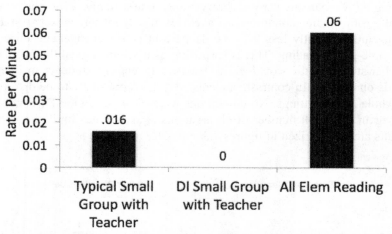

Figure 7.4   Disruptions Observed across Direct Instruction and Typical Reading Instruction

Opportunities to Respond across Instructional Delivery Methods

Another variable under which the provision of opportunities to respond can be analyzed is the method of instructional delivery being utilized. Data was sorted to determine and separate those instructional sessions in the content area of reading instruction that were determined to be small group (i.e., at least 90 percent of observed time spent in groups of six or fewer students

Table 7.1 Teacher-Provided Opportunities to Respond per Minute and (Average Wait Time in Minutes between OTRs) across Instructional Delivery Methods

Instructional Delivery Method	Group OTR	Individual OTR	Total OTR/min
All elementary reading	0.71	0.01	0.72
	(1:25)	*(100:00)*	*(1:23)*
Small-group reading* (>90%)	1.29	0.93	2.22
	(00:47)	*(1:05)*	*(00:27)*
Direct Instruction reading	9.86	0.36	10.22
	00:06	*(2:47)*	*(00:06)*

*Defined by observations in which at least 90 percent of the observed time was spent in small-group instruction (six or fewer students working with the teacher as a group).

working with the teacher), and those that implemented a Direct Instruction model. Observations were analyzed in terms of group, individual, and total opportunities to respond across the different instructional delivery methods. Table 7.1 summarizes this data.

The most obvious finding from this data is that instruction in reading using Direct Instruction methodology resulted in increased numbers of opportunities to respond when compared to small-group reading instruction and all elementary reading instruction. In fact, this is the first data that indicates the provision of opportunities to respond at targeted levels with Direct Instruction reading teachers providing 10.22 total opportunities per minute. This compares to 0.72 per minute with all elementary reading and 2.22 with small-group reading.

Another major finding is that individual opportunities to respond were delivered at low rates across all delivery methods with a range of 0.01 per minute in all elementary reading instruction to 0.93 in small-group reading—with Direct Instruction in the middle at 0.36. Group opportunities were considerably higher, especially with Direct Instruction reading with a rate of 9.86 per minute. Wait times for opportunities also was noticeably low with Direct Instruction with a six-second wait time with Direct Instruction reading group opportunities and total opportunities to respond. This is likely due to the type of interactive instruction typically seen in reading instruction.

Feedback across Instructional Delivery Methods

The degree to which a teacher is able to provide frequent feedback is dependent upon how often students are asked to respond during instruction. Thus, the teacher's provision of opportunities for student responding during instruction (as discussed in chapter 4) not only increases student engagement but also provides the teacher with increased opportunities for feedback. This logic begs a question as to whether varying instructional methods are associated with differential rates of those teacher behaviors that are known to promote student engagement and achievement.

Overall, teachers using Direct Instruction were observed to provide positive feedback at a rate more than 45 times that of typical reading and 16.4
times that of typical small-group reading. What's interesting is that teachers'
delivery of negative feedback holds fairly constant across all reading instruction. However, because of the elevated rates of positive feedback, students in
the Direct Instruction groups received positive-to-negative feedback at a ratio
of 64:1—a dramatic difference from typical reading instruction. These results
are summarized in table 7.2 and figure 7.5.

**Table 7.2   Feedback Types as Rates per Minute and *Average Number of Minutes
between Feedback* across all Elementary Reading Observations, Small-Group Reading
Observations, and Direct Instruction Reading Groups**

	Positive Feedback	Negative Feedback	Ratio of Positive to Negative
All elementary reading	0.10	0.05	0.2:1
	10:00	*20:00*	
Small-group reading* (>90%)	0.276	0.062	6:1
	3:36	*16:07*	
Direct Instruction reading	4.53	0.07	64:1
	00:32	*14:16*	

*Defined by observations in which at least 90 percent of the observed time was spent in small-group instruc-
tion (six or fewer students working with the teacher as a group).

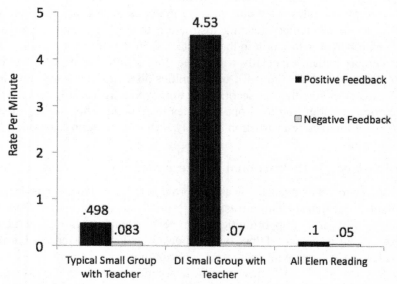

Figure 7.5   Teacher Feedback Rates across Direct Instruction and Typical Reading Instruction

IMPLICATIONS FOR EDUCATION

Due to a narrow definition of the methods in the original Institutional Review Board protocol, teacher identification and interviews were not included—an omission that needs to be corrected in future research efforts. Without this information it's difficult to determine whether teachers' consistently minimal use of effective practices is the result of skill deficits (don't know what to do), performance deficits (not fluent with practices), or compliance deficits (know how and can do but choose not to). What is clear is that teachers generally believe research to be irrelevant and untrustworthy (Broekkamp & van Hout-Woulters, 2007).

The fact that the main purveyors of instruction do not trust our current pedagogical science is cause for concern. In the absence of empirical evaluations of the relative effects of instructional practices on student outcomes, all practices are essentially equal. Or at best, practices are judged on criteria not related to effect—perhaps which is most comfortable or familiar. An example of this phenomenon is the continued widespread criticism of positive feedback (e.g., Kohn, 1999, 2001) despite the overwhelming evidence in its favor (e.g., Cameron & Pierce, 2002; Hattie, 2013; Strain & Joseph, 2004).

If as a field we agree that some strategies are more effective than others, then we must agree on a standard for making this determination. As discussed in chapter 1, an effect size—the degree to which an intervention moves the average students in relation to the entire population—is a logical manner of comparing instructional practices and strategies.

Implications for Teacher Training

Again, it is a given that not all practices are equal—some work better than others in terms of facilitating student success. While many practices may produce positive effects, some do so in a more effective or efficient manner. We can't judge the worth of a practice solely by the effect, as we can't assume that the ends can justify the means. Rather, we have to be concerned with comparison among acceptable interventions—assessing what practices provide the greatest benefit with the least cost.

Large-scale meta-analyses have clearly identified teacher practices that produce the largest effects (Hattie, 2013; Korpershoek, Harms, de Boer, van Kuijk, & Doolaard, 2016). But these practices are not typically the focus of teacher education (Kirschner, Sweller, & Clark, 2006). Rather, teacher preparation at the university level tends toward less-structured instruction, insisting that the student bear the main responsibility through inquiry or problem-based learning. Importantly, John Hattie (2013) has reported the effect size for inquiry-based learning at .31, problem-based learning at .16, and whole language reading programs at .06. In contrast, the effect size for Direct Instruction is reported at .57 and teaching students to solve problems is at .61.

Clearly, some things work better than others—but teacher education appears to have as much distrust of research as do teachers. As a case in point, there is overwhelming evidence for teaching behavioral expectations, active supervision of students, and encouraging positive behavior (Stronge, Ward, & Grant, 2011). However, in one large survey of teacher education universities in a large mid-western state, 42 percent did not teach prospective teachers about teaching behavior, 65 percent did not teach about active supervision, and 19 percent did not teach about encouragement for positive behavior (Oliver & Reschly, 2010).

There is little reason to believe that preservice teachers will adopt practices and strategies that were not introduced during their training. While there is room for teachers to find a comfort level with their own teaching style, there are foundational practices that must become a part of how we define teaching. The overwhelming majority of educational research identifies student engagement as a major predictor of success. At a minimum, teachers must understand that it is their responsibility to create this engagement. But simply telling adults is no more effective than telling students, instruction requires repetition with guidance and feedback.

Education would do well to consider teaching as a skill to be taught to prospective teachers through the same set of practices that are foundational for teaching children. Prospective teachers should receive a rationale for each practice and be aware of the research. Practices should then be introduced and modeled by teacher education faculty who have mastered the content—gradually leading new teachers to practice with guidance until their own mastery has been reached. Stated as directly and succinctly as possible, students (adults and children) who are not taught simply have a less chance of success both now and in the future.

Implications for Schools

Because teachers often enter the profession with a lack of knowledge of basic foundational practices, much of what teachers come to rely on is learned on the job during their first years in the profession. Novice teachers report that classroom management is their top challenge (American Psychological Association, 2006). Unfortunately, in the absence of tried and true strategies, these inexperienced teachers more often resort to exclusion—sending students away from instruction or even out of the classroom (Banks & Zionts, 2009).

While there are a variety of factors influencing student success in school, teachers through their practice have a major impact on the probability of that success (Stronge et al., 2011). For example, Rockoff (2004) reports that a one standard deviation increase in teacher quality raises test scores by approximately .20 standard deviations in reading and .24 standard deviations in math. Further, Chetty, Friedman, and Rockoff (2014) found that raising the quality of teaching from the bottom 5 percent to just average raises predicted student lifetime income by $250,000.

Continuous Professional Growth Model

An effective professional growth model is supported by the same logic that we know is effective for any effort to change systemic practice. Participants must be provided with clear definitions, entertaining rationale, realistic examples with opportunities for discussion, and a process of collaborative coaching and feedback to build mastery. It is recommended that teams or professional learning communities within the school meet regularly to focus on consistent improvement and the development of a climate of excellence in the school. This model is presented in figure 7.6.

Logic

As a first step, teachers need to be introduced to a logic that helps them to (1) understand the challenges, (2) visualize a logic for change, (3) be familiar with the evidence for a solution, and (4) be exposed to the structure for getting there (Garmston & Wellman, 2013). This begins with a clear description of the challenges facing students and the evidence for effective practices. The goal is to make this introduction brief, informative, and entertaining— keeping teachers interested as they are introduced to the content.

Discrimination

Once teachers are familiar with the concepts, video-based or role-played scenarios are presented to help with discrimination of the key features of the

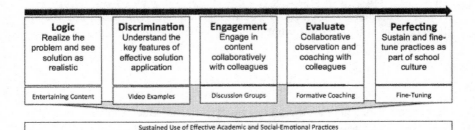

Figure 7.6 The L-DEEP Professional Growth Model

effective practices. Both positive and negative examples across a wide range of student ages and cultures are presented with attention called to the key features of the effective practices being discussed.

Engagement

A thorough understanding of each practice leads directly to a structured discussion among teachers in grade-level/content-area teams or professional learning communities. These small groups will consider deeper content in additional videos or role-play vignettes and discuss challenges and strategies for application. This collaborative and engaging discussion among professionals is a crucial component of any sustainable professional development.

Evaluation

Teachers leave their collaborative engagement sessions with plans to coach and be coached by other team members as part of an ongoing practice and feedback loop. Procedures for collaborative coaching will be presented and demonstrated so that all teachers receive monthly observations from peers and use the resulting feedback to engage in continuous improvement.

Perfecting

Effective professional development has no end. Rather, teachers become better at coaching one another and continue to work toward perfecting strategies across a wider range of students and conditions. Further, effective practices identified as part of the collaborative coaching process should become the focus on administrator walk-through evaluations, helping to make practices a part of the school culture.

Overall, the keys to effective professional growth are in the selection of high-probability strategies and practices, continuous engagement of faculty throughout the year and over a career, and formative feedback on progress toward a goal. Clearly, however, like any effective school-wide effort, the school leadership must encourage, support, and evaluate teacher efforts as a serious component of the school's culture. The issue cannot be simple compliance; it must be a part of what it means to be an effective teacher.

CONCLUSIONS

Like most social sciences, there are no certainties in education, only probabilities. We don't know that supervising students will result in fewer fights, but we know the probabilities favor it. Similarly, we don't know that modeling for students, engaging them during instruction, or providing frequent feedback will enhance success—but we do know that these strategies increase, if not maximize, the probabilities.

The fact that teachers were found here to use effective practices at very low rates was not totally surprising. The literature has alluded to this fact for decades. Despite the deficits, there is reason for hope as we do know what our most effective or high-probability practices are—we just have to increase the fidelity and frequency of their use. Finding that students are failing at unacceptable rates while observing that teachers using high-probability practices at high rates would be a much darker outcome as it does not prescribe a solution.

As a field, education must push forward with a science of pedagogy and instruction that is focused on practices and strategies that have been demonstrated to provide the highest probabilities for success. For now, simply moving our teaching force to provide more engagement, more feedback, and better management would very likely produce significant gains.

Classroom Observation
Training Manual

TRAINING AND *RELIABILITY PROCEDURE*

Use the following strategy to train data collectors to become reliable.

- Go over CODE DEFINITIONS and CODING RULES daily. This will enforce the definitions and rules so there will not be a tendency to stray from the established system. Everyone is prone to observer drift and studying the definitions and rules daily will help with accuracy.
- Start with short sessions of observations using the training DVD. With each scenario, the target student will have a red box to indicate which student is the target. The screen will present a five-second countdown to start. Have all students collect data at the same time.
- On first practice session, have data collectors watch the classroom scenario without attempting to collect data. As events occur, the trainer should call out the appropriate code. Stop the DVD if necessary to discuss why certain events would be coded in the way called out. Areas that data coders typically need practice recognizing are correction, negative feedback, and OTR group.
- After watching two scenarios and calling out the appropriate codes, have data collectors code the behaviors using a paper and pencil format. After each scenario, check the recorded data for reliability.
- Continue to practice on the two familiar scenarios until the data collectors have achieved 80 percent reliability. Once they have achieved 80 percent reliability, have them code the two scenarios using the handheld PDA (personal digital assistant) and MOOSES (Multi-Option Observation System for Experimental Studies) software. After each scenario, print out the recorded codes and talk through the data line by line. Compute reliability.

Once data collectors have achieved 80 percent reliability, have them record data using the two scenarios they have not observed. Once they have achieved 80 percent reliability on the second set of scenarios, they are ready to begin training with live observations.

- Start with short sessions of live observations, approximately ten minutes. If there is difficulty getting reliable, shorten the session to five minutes. In between each session, leave the observation area and talk through the data line by line immediately following that particular session.
- Try to do as many short sessions in the time allocated. In a thirty-minute period, you should be able to get at least four five-minute sessions in with a discussion in between. The more sessions scored will increase the chances of becoming reliable across all codes in a more reasonable time frame.
- Immediately after the coding session, run the interobserver agreement. This will aid in seeing some weaknesses. During this period an *error analysis* needs to be done on each session that is not reliable so that the problem areas are even more magnified. Brainstorming on examples, going over tapes, and studying the code definitions can emphasize concentration on these codes.

PROTOCOL FOR DATA COLLECTION

1. *Each time you collect data, you will need a **handheld PDA computer and a folder with post-it notes.** Always check your handheld power supply before leaving the office. If it is necessary to use the adapter, ask the school staff quietly if you can access an outlet and still remain close to the target.*

2. *Arrive early enough to the observation site to determine the most optimal place to sit. Position yourself in close proximity to the target student so you can hear what is said and you have a clear vision of student behavior and activity. If you are taking reliability with another coder, consider where to position both of you without affecting the flow of the classroom and regularly occurring activities. Try not to disturb the normal interactions of the environment. After the initial visit, you do not need talk to the staff upon entering the environment (unless you need specific information). It is okay to acknowledge staff; however, you should not engage him or her in a conversation or disturb the site flow. The same holds true for the target student and peers as well. You can expect peers to be curious about your presence, but DO NOT talk to them at length. If a peer tries to engage you, politely tell him or her that you cannot talk right then, that you have work to do.*

3. *Enter/exit the area as inconspicuously as possible. Avoid taking extra items (not required for data collection) with you, and make sure that you have all the necessary materials prior to entering the room. Never respond to student behavior (e.g., laughing). Similarly, you should not respond when negative things occur such as staff-administered punishment or acts of aggression. We are strictly observing events as they happen and do not want our actions in any way to resemble judgment or criticism. If you are disturbed by what you have observed, you may discuss it with us, but no one else.*
4. *After you are situated in the environment, turn on your handheld and begin collecting data.*

A Few Miscellaneous Things…

Always be on time—remember that we are guests and are there at the convenience of staff. If you are going to be late, you should call the site to let the staff know. Phone the project coordinator at the earliest possible time (i.e., the night before) if you are unable to come to work due to illness or an emergency so we can try to find a replacement for your scheduled sessions.

Confidentiality   Remember that we have **GUARANTEED** confidentiality to all participants in the study. You should never discuss anything with anyone other than project staff. It is never appropriate to identify participants in the study to others or to discuss what you have observed during the course of the study. It is also imperative that we remain prompt, courteous, and cooperative with the staff of the study.

STEPS FOR USING MINI-MOOSES

1. Turn on handheld using power button on upper right-hand side.
2. Using the stylus choose **Start** and then **MiniMoose3**.
3. Choose **File** (bottom left-hand corner of screen) and **New File**.
4. Using the document, *CARS File Name Codes* follow the steps to name the 20-digit file name.
5. On the same screen choose **Folder** and *"Your Name* Data File" (e.g., Parish Data File) and then **Save**.
6. Under the **Header** line write "one" or "mul" depending on the number of teachers in your room and then click **OK** UNLESS you are coding a reliability observation. If so, in the Header line the primary observer opens the keyboard (middle of the screen), adds one space, and puts "pri." If the observer is not the primary observer code, "rel."

7. Slide the bottom cursor to the right fill in the demographic information. Double check.
8. Before the coding session begins choose the Whole Group, Passive Engagement, and Teach as the default.
9. From the lower part of the screen choose **Timer**. When coding with a partner count down, "3-2-1-**Start**."
10. When the observation is up at fifteen minutes, in the middle of the screen a box appears that states that the session is over. In the upper right corner of that box click on "OK."
11. On the bottom left of the screen choose **File** and then **Exit**.
12. Your observation file is now saved.

DIRECTIONS FOR SENDING DATA FILES

1. Using the USB cord, attach the handheld to your computer.
2. When the *Windows Mobile Devise Center* Screen appears, choose:Connect without setting up your device
3. From the options given choose:**File Management** and thenBrowse the contents of your device
4. After locating the data files to be sent, drag them onto your desktop. Exit out of the Windows Mobile Devise and disconnect handheld.
5. Open and compose an email to Regina Hirn (regina.hirn@louisville.edu) attaching the necessary data files.
6. When sending observations, in the subject line write: School Name **Data Files**. For example, Milton Data Files. If sending a reliability file, in the subject line write *School Name Reliability—MP & NS*.
7. Do not attach both reliability files and data files in the same email to Regina. First send your data files and then in a separate email send your reliabilities.
8. If possible send all observations to Regina Hirn the same day they were completed.
9. If you had to use the FIX key during an observation clean up the file before sending it. Fixing a file:
   a. On the handheld open Office Mobile
   b. Choose Word Mobile
   c. Select file that needs to be fixed
   d. Find the word FIX and delete the code before the word as well as the word FIX
   e. Choose OK

DIRECT OBSERVATION CODES

Instruction Variables

Mutually Exclusive
At least one field must be toggled on

"Whole Gr"

Whole group is defined as the target student being expected to participate in an activity that involves the majority or the entire class and in which the teacher is providing the students with direct instruction in academic content (e.g., reading, math, science lesson; social skills group). If target student is not participating due to timeout or some other disciplinary action taken by the teacher, score the activity as whole group.

Examples:

All students are listening to a teacher lecture.

All students are doing a math worksheet with the teacher (even if given a few minutes between instructions to complete item).

Nonexamples:

Teacher has completed instruction and has directed students to complete the assignment on their own.

Resource or pull-out service (if less than 10):

If class is less than 10 code SG Teach.

"SG Peer"

Small group peer is defined as the target student being expected to participate with one or more peers without being teacher directed. During this activity, the students are discussing, collaborating, and working together without the teacher.

Examples:

Target and three peers are asked to discuss a topic for a few minutes.

Target and a peer work together on a lab activity.

Students break up into pairs to work on math jeopardy.

Nonexample:

Students are working together in small groups yet the target student has been assigned an independent task (leave as ind).

RULE:

Only change to "Sm-G Teach" if teacher is **leading** the instruction not if they stop by and listen-in, or monitor.

"SG Teach"	Small group teacher is defined as the target student being expected to participate in a group with a portion of the students in the class (at least one other student) and an adult. During this activity the adult is providing the students in the group with **direct** instruction. Code resource rooms with SG Teach as most of them have 10 students or less.

Examples:

Subset of class (that includes target) is following an academic lesson led by the teacher at a table in the back of the room.

Instructional groups where students share a common activity but different tasks with different instructions about what to do led by teacher.

Students are divided into cooperative learning groups led by teacher.

Groups are located at work or interest stations in the room, each of which is devoted to a different activity, with different tasks, and different instructions about what to do with a teacher.

Nonexample:

Target student asks a peer a task-related question or looks at the work of the peer. |
| "Ind Wrk" | Independent work is defined as the target student being expected to sit at his or her seat (on the floor, at the blackboard) and work independently. This may include reading, completing worksheets, and taking a test.

Example:

Each student working on academic tasks by themselves for seatwork with no teacher instruction.

Target student is engaged in individual study.

Target student is using the computer without teacher directions.

Independent Reading

Nonexample:

Teacher is working over the shoulder of the target student helping them with a problem. (Code as "One-on-One") |

"1-on-1"

No five-second count/code as starts and stops

One-on-one is defined as the target student being provided individual direct instruction or attention in academic content by an adult. Code "**1-on-1**" immediately; do not wait for the five-second count.

Examples:

A teacher and the target student are working on a PowerPoint together.

The target student ONLY is receiving feedback from the teacher about a worksheet they just completed.

Spanish teacher comes alongside student and quizzes vocabulary.

Nonexamples:

Teacher conducting a round robin with geography facts in whole group.

Teacher is playing trivia jeopardy with the class where the teacher stops on one student for a period of time exchanging dialogue in efforts to clarify their response. (Code as OTR individual during whole group)

Positive/negative feedback or corrections.

Teacher Observation Variables

Mutually Exclusive	Descriptor	Definition
At least one variable for each field must be toggled on	Teaching DEFAULT	Teacher is engaged in instruction by explaining a concept, demonstrating a principle, or modeling a skill or activity to group that includes target student. The teaching must be academic and furthering the lesson/objective of class. Eyes on students. Instructing/modeling/monitoring.
		Examples:
		Teacher is lecturing to the whole class during a history lesson.
		Teacher is oriented at the front of the class overseeing a video being shown.
		Teacher is demonstrating how to perform a lab assignment to the whole class.
		Teacher is working with target student on explaining a concept where the target student simply nods or gestures.
		Teacher is giving directions to a small group of individuals on what sequence of events need to be accomplished and presented on for the group project.
		Operating PowerPoint or writing on board.
		Teacher stops and briefly talks with various students around the room asking how they are doing; if they need any help, providing feedback.
		Nonexamples:
		Teacher is asking class about weekend plans.
		Teacher is talking about a basketball player and the great plays he made at last night's game.
		Teacher is on the phone.
		Teacher is working on the computer.
		Teacher steps out of the classroom to speak to another teacher.

	Not teaching	Teacher is not engaging students and is involved in independent task with no interactions with student. Use "Not-teach" when teacher is talking off-topic or reprimanding another student for more than five seconds. *Examples:* *Students working in small groups or independently while teacher works at desk or on computer or other task.* *Teacher is asking about Friday night's basketball game.* *Teacher is working on computer at his or her desk.* *Teacher is on the phone with eyes away from the class.* *Nonexample:* *Teacher is reading chapters from novel out loud to class.*
Frequency counts	OTR group	Teacher (or tutor) provides an opportunity to respond that is curriculum relevant that is directed at whole class or small group that includes the target student. OTR must be instruction related and not a social question, a question within the context of negative feedback or a direction to perform a task. This question is not rhetorical or instructional. Students must have to think about answering the question. OTR must be relevant to curriculum. **Teacher is asking a question related to lesson. Provides a task with curricular insight.** *Examples:* *Teacher asks questions and looks for volunteer to answer, for example, "Who can list three events that took place just prior to the invasion of Normandy?" "Is Sudan a landlocked country?" "I am thinking of two specific precious metals that are found in this area, who can help me find an answer?"* *Teacher asks questions as above yet specifies a group that target student is in, "Can someone from group 1 tell me the answer?"* *Nonexamples:* *Teacher tells students to get out their math book.* *Teacher calls on several students by name other than the target student.* *Teacher asks, "Didn't you all hear me ask for quiet?"* *Teacher asks a question to a small group that doesn't include the target student.*

OTR individual

Teacher provides an opportunity to respond that is directed to target student. OTR must be instruction related and not a social question or a question within the context of negative feedback. This OTR must be curriculum drive. **Teacher asks a question to the target student related to the lesson.**

Examples:

"Lyle, explain the difference between a sedimentary and an igneous rock."

"Mike, tell me how to work this algebra problem."

"Ian, what branch of government is responsible for making laws?"

"Please explain further your rationale, Grace."

Nonexamples:

Teacher asks questions and looks for volunteer to answer, for example, "Who can list three events that took place just prior to the invasion of Normandy?" "Is Sudan a landlocked country?" "I am thinking of two specific precious metals that are found in this area, who can help me find an answer?" (OTR Group)

Teacher calls for volunteers and target has hand up yet doesn't get called on. (Code as OTR Group & Get Attention)

Teacher asks, "Did you have to work last night?"

Teacher asks, "What did you do this weekend?"

Direction

Teacher provides a direction command that is directed at whole class or small group that includes the target student. Direction is not related to the contents of the class curriculum but to specific behavioral commands. Direction is an immediate command, no "if" or "when" statements. **A task with no insight.**

Examples:

Sit down and get a pencil out.

Take out your book and turn to page 14.

Go get your lunch.

Look up at the agenda on the board.

Nonexamples:

Who can tell me why Melinda didn't get along with Rachel?

What part of this formula am I missing?

Think about this.... Listen to this...

Turn to page 14 and put your finger on the word that begins with L.

Positive feedback GO Command	Teacher gives the class or individual student feedback on an academic or social behavior that indicates the behavior/response is correct. Can be verbal or gestural. *Examples:* *"Students who are copying down the objective and outline are showing they know how to get the task started, I respect their independence."* *"Thanks for submitting the assignment; I'm pleased to see it."* *"Everyone was in their seat and working on the warm-up problem when the bell rang, I appreciate your responsible self-management."* *"Thanks for raising your hand first."* *Great job!* *"4"—Acknowledging that 4 was the correct answer.* *Nonexamples:* *"Yes, you're right" to another student.*
Negative feedback STOP Command	Teacher informs student that behavior/response is incorrect, but does not provide corrective feedback (e.g., "no" "stop that" "turn around" "quiet"). Can be verbal or gestural. *Examples:* *A teacher puts finger to lips and says, "SHH!"* *"Stop bothering Kim."* *"I told you to sit down."* *Teacher raises her finger to her mouth to gesture students to be quiet.* *Teacher asks Jan to "have a seat" when Jane gets of her seat during independent seatwork.* *Teacher takes pencil/iPod/cell phone away from student who is playing with it and not following instructions.* *No—telling the student that the academic answer he or she gave was wrong.* *Nonexamples:* *"Try harder on your math worksheet; I know you can do better."* *Students come in to class after fire drill and teacher asks them to "take a seat."* *"I want everyone's attention while I go over this example."*

Correct *STOP & GO* *Command*	Teacher tells student why behavior/response is not correct and re-teaches correct behavior/response. *Examples:* *Number 24 is wrong; can you look at it again and try again?* *"Barbara, I see that you are texting on your cell phone; the school policy on cell phone use is clear. The phone should only be out at lunch and after 2:30."* *"Shalita, you know that sleeping is not acceptable I my class, therefore what I would like to see you do if you have a question is ask me or a peer that you're working with for the answer."* *"Victor, you know that we don't use those words in this class. A more appropriate response to get my attention would be to raise your hand or say Mrs. Smith, can you help me with this problem I am having difficulty with."* *"Do not throw your garbage away from across the room. If you need to throw something away while I am lecturing feel free to get up and walk over to the waste basket."* *Put that away and read your novel.* *Leave him alone and get back to work.* *Nonexamples:* *"You know better than that."* *"Get busy."* *Stop it! I've told you this twice already!*
Acknowledge	Teacher answers question **or** acknowledges the student. Teacher responds to query from student, either academic or social. **Teacher can respond in a nonverbal way.** *Examples:* *Teacher points to target student who has hand raised in response to OTR group.* *Teacher answers student question about what time it is.* *Nonexamples:* *Teacher tells student to be quiet.* *Teacher asks target student an instructionally related question (OTR Indiv.).*

Student Observation Variables

Mutually Exclusive	Descriptor	Definition
At least one variable must be toggled on	S Act Eng	Student Active Engagement: Student is actively engaging with instructional content via choral response, raising hand, responding to teacher instruction, writing, reading, or otherwise completing assigned task.
		Examples:
		Target student is writing on an assigned worksheet page.
		Target student is reading out loud with the class when directed to do so, following along with finger or eyes in text.
		Target student is working on the computer-assigned task from the teacher.
		Target student is working in assigned group helping to complete a task.
		Watching a movie shown by teacher.
		Nonexamples:
		Student is watching or listening.
		Target student is oriented toward the teacher or speaker and appears to be following instruction or course of events.
		Student is sleeping.
	S Pass Eng*SET AS DEFAULT	Student Passive Engagement: Student is passively attending to instruction by orientation to teacher or peer if appropriate.
		Examples:
		Student is listening to lecture or watching presentation including PWPT or video.
		Student looks and listens to another student called on.
		Head down on desk yet eyes oriented to teacher.
		Target student is oriented toward the teacher or speaker and appears to be following instruction or course of events.
		Nonexamples:
		Student has head down yet not looking at teacher.
		Student is reading silently. (Code as Act Eng)
		Student looks and listens to a student talking off-task topic.

S Off task	Student is neither actively engaged nor looking at the teacher but is not disrupting the class in any way (no negative behaviors). *Examples:* *Target student is out of seat without permission but not bothering anyone else.* *Target student looking away from the teacher or instructional materials.* *Target student not complying with a request (e.g., to open books, to look at board, to write an answer, and does not appear to be thinking about the answer to write).* *Target student has head down on desk with eyes closed.* *Target student is texting a friend.* *Target student is playing with iPod.* *Nonexamples:* *Student looks away and talks to peer for less than five seconds.* *Student silently watches video.*
Downtime	There are no academic expectations of the target student or group target student is part of. Use downtime any time a reprimand or discussion with another student exceeds five seconds without clear expectations. If student leaves class to go to the restroom/get a jacket/get her jacket, code Downtime. *Examples:* *At beginning or end of class no instruction has started and class is talking among themselves.* *Target student finishes an assignment or test and lays their head down as nothing else has been asked of him or her.* *Teacher is instructing and steps away to answer phone or speak to someone at door **without** informing students of what to do ("work on ... while I attend to this").* *Student leaves room with permission from teacher (use restroom/get a drink of water).* *Nonexamples:* *Teacher is lecturing and student is sleeping or has head down. (Off Task)* *Teacher is instructing and steps away to answer phone yet tells class to "go ahead and get a start on the project and I'll be right back."* *All class is waiting and talking prior to instruction yet target student gets homework out and completes.* *Teacher reprimands another student for more than five seconds yet tells class to "keep working while I talk to Tim."*

Frequency counts	Disruptive	Student is neither actively engaged nor displays behavior that does or potentially could disrupt the lesson (e.g., out of seat; noises, talking to peer, making comments). Behaviors can range from low intensity (out of seat to sharpen pencil) to high intensity (making derogatory statements or destroying property).

WHEN TO COUNT A NEW ONE:

Code new event if topography changes (i.e., talking and then tapping) or if talking changes to new person or if five seconds of pause or if other speaker (teacher or peer) respond then target talks again.

Examples:

Cell phone talking or any use with music/noise.

Argumentative or noncompliant talk.

Negative talk.

Target student is out of seat without permission and taking to peer.

Target student is ripping or crumbling paper in loud way drawing attention from teacher and/or peers.

Target student is making noise drawing attention from teacher and/or peers.

Target student curses teacher or peers.

Target student makes threatening comments to teacher or peers.

Target student verbally refuses to complete assignment or comply with directions.

Loudly tapping pen or rocking in chair to extent it is drawing attention or has potential to draw attention and disrupt instruction.

Nonexamples:

Just cell phone use for texting. (Code as off task)

Sleeping.

Laying head down.

Not answering when called on.

Quietly tapping pen or rocking in chair if not distracting or drawing attention.

Get attention	Student raises hand **or** asks question in an appropriate manner to elicit an answer (academic or social) from the teacher.

Examples:

Target student raises hand in class.

Target student asks the teacher for more paper.

Nonexamples:

Student says a derogatory comment about assignment. (DISRUPTIVE)

Student responds to the teachers OTR individual with a question.

References

Adams, G. R., & Cohen, A. S. (1974). Children's physical and interpersonal characteristics that effect student-teacher interactions. *Journal of Experimental Education, 43*(1), 1–5.

American Psychological Association. Coalition for Psychology in Schools and Education. (2006). *Report on the teacher needs survey.* Washing, DC: American Psychological Association. Center for Psychology in Schools and Education.

Banks, T., & Zionts, P. (2009). Teaching a cognitive behavioral strategy to manage emotions. *Intervention in School & Clinic, 44*(5), 307–313.

Berliner, D. C. (1990). What's all the fuss about instructional time? *The nature of time in schools: Theoretical concepts, practitioner perceptions.* New York: Teachers College, Columbia University.

Borich, G. D. (2011). *Observation skills for effective teaching.* Boston, MA: Pearson.

Bottiani, J. H., Bradshaw, C. P., Rosenberg, M. S., Hershfeldt, P. A., Pell, K. L., & Debnam, K. J. (2012). Applying Double Check to response to intervention: Culturally responsive practices for learning disabilities. *Insight on Learning Disabilities: Prevailing Theories to Validated Practices, 9*, 93–107.

Broekkamp, H., & van Hout-Wolters, B. (2007). The gap between educational research and practice: A literature review, symposium, and questionnaire. *Educational Research and Evaluation, 13*(3), 203–220.

Brophy, J. (2006). History of research on classroom management. In C. M. Evertson & C. S. Weinstein (Eds.), *Handbook of classroom management: Research, practice, and contemporary issues* (pp. 17–43). Mahwah, NJ: Erlbaum.

Brophy J., & Good, T. (1986). Teacher behavior and student achievement. In M. C. Wittrock (Ed.), *Handbook on research on teaching* (3rd ed., pp. 328–375). New York: Macmillan.

Busch, T. (1995). Gender differences in self-efficacy and attitudes toward computers. *Journal of Educational Computing Research, 12*(2), 147–158.

Cameron, J., & Pierce, W. D. (2002). *Rewards and intrinsic motivation: Resolving the controversy.* Westport, CT: Bergin and Garvey.

109

Chetty, R., Friedman, J. N., & Rockoff, J. E. (2014). Measuring the impacts of teachers I: Evaluating bias in teacher value-added estimates. *American Economic Review, 104*(9), 2593–2632.

Conroy, M. A., Sutherland, K. S., Snyder, A. L., & Marsh, S. (2008). Classwide interventions: Effective instruction makes a difference. *Teaching Exceptional Children, 40*, 24–30.

Cooper, J., Hirn, R. G., & Scott, T. M (2015). The teacher as change agent: Considering instructional practice to prevent student failure. *Preventing School Failure, 59*(1), 1–4. doi: 10.1080/1045988X.2014.919135

Dee, T. S. (2004). Teachers, race, and student achievement in a randomized experiment. *Review of Economics and Statistics, 86*(1), 195–210.

Dee, T. S. (2005). A teacher like me: Does race, ethnicity, or gender matter? *American Economic Review, 95*(2), 158–165.

Eddy, C. M., & Easton-Brooks, D. (2011). Ethnic matching, school placement, and mathematics achievement of African American students from kindergarten through fifth grade. *Urban Education, 46*(6), 1280–1299.

Egalite, A. J., Kisida, B., & Winters, M. A. (2015). Representation in the classroom: the effect of own-race teachers on student achievement. *Economics of Education Review, 45*, 44–52.

Ehrenberg, R. G., & Brewer, D. J. (1995). Did teachers' verbal ability and race matter in the 1960s? Coleman revisited. *Economics of Education Review, 14*, 1–21.

Ellis, E. S., & Worthington, L. A. (1994). *Research synthesis on effective teaching principles and the design of quality tools for educators* (Technical Report No. 5). Eugene: University of Oregon, National Center to Improve the Tools of Educators.

Engelmann, S. (2007). Student-program alignment and teaching to mastery. *Journal of Direct Instruction, 7*(1), 45–66.

Fendick, F. (1990). *The correlation between teacher clarify of communication and student achievement gain: A meta-analysis.* PhD dissertation, University of Florida.

Ferguson, R. F. (2003). Teachers' perceptions and expectations and the Black-White test score gap. *Urban Education, 38*(4), 460–507.

Fredrickson, B. L. (1998). What good are positive emotions? *Review of General Psychology, 2*(3), 300–319.

Garmston, R. J., & Wellman, B. M. (2013). *The adaptive school: A sourcebook for developing collaborative groups.* Rowman & Littlefield.

Gersten, R. M., Darch, C., & Gleason, M. (1988). Effectiveness of a Direct Instruction academic kindergarten for low-income students. *Elementary School Journal, 89*, 227–240.

Graham, S. (Ed.). (2005). Criteria for evidence-based practice in special education [Special issue]. *Exceptional Children, 71*(2).

Greenwood, C. R., Horton, B. T., & Utley, C. A. (2002). Academic engagement: Current perspectives in research and practice. *School Psychology Review, 31*, 328–349.

Gunter, P. L., Denny, R. K., Jack, S. L., Shores, R. E., & Nelson, C. M. (1993). Aversive stimuli in academic interactions between students with serious emotional disturbance and their teachers. *Behavioral Disorders, 18*(4), 265–274.

Hattie, J. (2009). *Visible learning: A synthesis of over 800 meta-analyses relating to achievement.* New York: Routledge.

Hattie, J. (2013). *Visible learning: A synthesis of over 800 meta-analyses relating to achievement*. New York: Routledge.

Hattie, J. A. C., & Timperley, H. (2007). The power of feedback. *Review of Educational Research, 77*(1), 81–112.

Haydon, T., Conroy, M., Scott, T. M., Sindelar, P., Barber, B. R., & Orlando, A. (2010). Comparison of three types of opportunities to respond on student academic and social behaviors. *Journal of Emotional and Behavioral Disorders, 18*(1), 27–40.

Hirn, R. G., & Scott, T. M. (2014). Descriptive analysis of teacher instructional practices and student engagement among adolescents with and without challenging behavior. *Education and Treatment of Children, 37*(4), 585–607.

Howsen, R. M., & Trawick, M. W. (2007). Teachers, race and student achievement revisited. *Applied Economics Letters, 14*, 1023–1027.

Huebner, E. S. (1991). Initial development of the student's life satisfaction scale. *School Psychology International, 12*(3), 231–240.

Jones, M. G., Howe, A., & Rua, M. J. (2000). Gender differences in students' experiences, interests, and attitudes toward science and scientists. *Science Education, 84*(2), 180–192.

Kida, T. (2006). *Don't believe everything you think: The 6 basic mistakes we make in thinking*. Amherst, NY: Prometheus Books.

Kidron, Y., & Lindsay, J. (2014). The effects of increased learning time on student academic and nonacademic outcomes: Findings from a meta-analytic review. REL 2014-015. *Regional Educational Laboratory Appalachia*.

Kirschner, P. A., Sweller, J., & Clark, R. E. (2006). Why minimal guidance during instruction does not work: An analysis of the failure of constructivist, discovery, problem-based, experiential, and inquiry-based teaching. *Educational Psychologist, 41*(2), 75–86.

Klassen, R. M., & Chiu, M. M. (2010). Effects on teachers' self-efficacy and job satisfaction: Teacher gender, years of experience, and job stress. *Journal of Educational Psychology, 102*(3), 741.

Kohn, A. (1999). *Punished by rewards* (2nd ed.). New York: Mariner Books.

Kohn, A. (2001). Five reasons to stop saying, "good job!" *Young Children, 56*(5), 24–30.

Konstantopoulos, S., & Chung, V. (2011). The persistence of teacher effects in elementary grades. *American Educational Research Journal, 48*(2), 361–386.

Korpershoek, H., Harms, T., de Boer, H., van Kuijk, M., & Doolaard, S. (2016). A meta-analysis of the effects of classroom management strategies and classroom management programs on students' academic, behavioral, emotional, and motivational outcomes. *Review of Educational Research, 86*(3), 643–680.

Losen, D. J., & Skiba, R. J. (2010). *Suspended education: Urban middle schools in crisis*. Montgomery, AL: Southern Poverty Law Center.

MacSuga-Gage, A. S., & Simonsen, B. (2015). Examining the effects of teacher-directed opportunities to respond on student outcomes: A systematic review of the literature. *Education and Treatment of Children, 38*, 211–244.

McGrady, P. B., & Reynolds, J. R. (2013). Racial mismatch in the classroom: Beyond black-white differences. *Sociology of Education, 86*(1), 3–17.

McIntosh, K., Chard, D., Boland, J., & Horner, R. H. (2006). A demonstration of combined efforts in school-wide academic and behavioral systems and incidence of reading and behavior challenges in early elementary grades. *Journal of Positive Behavior Interventions, 8*, 146–154.

Mickelson, R. A. (2001). Subverting Swann: First- and second-generation segregation in the Charlotte-Mecklenburg schools. *American Educational Research Journal, 38*, 215–252.

Mooney, C., & Kirshenbaum, S. (2009). *Unscientific America: How scientific illiteracy threatens our future.* New York: Basic Books.

National Center for Educational Statistics. (2015). *National Assessment of Educational Progress: School composition and the Black-White achievement gap.* Washington DC: National Center for Education Statistics.

National Institute of Child Health and Human Development, National Institute for Literacy, US Department of Education. (2001). *Put reading first: The research building blocks for teaching children to read.* Washington DC: US Government Printing Office.

National Mathematics Advisory Panel. (2008). *Foundation for success: The final report of the national mathematics advisory panel.* Washington, DC: US Department of Education.

Nickerson, R. S. (1998). Confirmation bias: A ubiquitous phenomenon in many guises. *Review of General Psychology, 2*(2), 175–220. doi: 10.1037/1089-2680.2.2.175

No Child Left Behind Act of 2001, Pub. L. No. 107-110.

Nye, B., Konstantopoulos, S., & Hedges, L. V. (2004). How large are teacher effects? *Educational Evaluation and Policy Analysis, 26*(3), 237–257.

Oliver, R. M., & Reschly, D. J. (2010). Special education teacher preparation in classroom management: Implications for students with emotional and behavioral disorders. *Behavioral Disorders, 35*(3), 188–199.

Pajares, F., & Valiante, G. (1999). Grade level and gender differences in the writing self-beliefs of middle school students. *Contemporary Educational Psychology, 24*(4), 390–405.

Peirce, C. S. (1877). The fixation of belief. *Popular Science Monthly, 12,* 1–15. Reprinted online at *Peirce.org,* http://www.pierce.org/writings/p107/html. Retrieved July 12, 2010.

Pianta, R. C. (1996). *High-risk children in schools: Constructing sustaining relationships.* New York: Routledge.

Pianta, R. C., Belsky, J., Vandergrift, N., Houts, R., & Morrison, F. J. (2008). Classroom effects on children's achievement trajectories in elementary school. *American Educational Research Journal, 45*(2), 365–397.

Rausch, M. K., & Skiba, R. (2004). Disproportionality in school discipline among minority students in Indiana: Description and analysis. Children Left Behind Policy Briefs. Supplementary Analysis 2-A. *Center for Evaluation and Education Policy, Indiana University.*

Reid, R., Gonzalez, J. E., Nordness, P. D., Trout, A., & Epstein, M. H. (2004). A meta-analysis of the academic status of students with emotional/behavioral disturbance. *Journal of Special Education, 38*(3), 130–143.

Rivkin, S. G., Hanushek, E. A., & Kain, J. F. (2005). Teachers, schools, and academic achievement. *Econometrica, 73*(2), 417–458.

Rockoff, J. E. (2004). The impact of individual teachers on student achievement: Evidence from panel data. *American Economic Review, 94*(2), 247–252.

Rocque, M., & Paternoster, R. (2011). Understanding the antecedents of the" school-to-jail" link: The relationship between race and school discipline. *Journal of Criminal Law and Criminology*, 633–665.

Rosenshine, B. (1986). Synthesis of research on explicit teaching. *Educational Leadership, 43*, 60–69.

Rosenshine, B., & Stevens, R. (1986). Teaching functions. In M. Wittrock (Ed.), *Handbook of research on teaching* (3rd ed.). New York: Macmillan.

Sackett, D. (1996). Evidence-based medicine—What it is and what it isn't. *British Medical Journal, 312*, 71–72. Retrieved from http://www.bmj.com/cgi/content/full/312/7023/71

Schwarzer, R., & Hallum, S. (2008). Perceived teacher self-efficacy as a predictor of job stress and burnout: Mediation analyses. *Applied Psychology, 57*(s1), 152–171.

Scruggs, T. E., & Mastropieri, M. A. (Eds.). (2009). *Policy and practice: Advances in learning and behavior disabilities* (vol. 22). Bingly, England: Emerald.

Simonsen, B., Fairbanks, S., Briesch, A., Myers, D., & Sugai, G. (2008). Evidence-based practices in classroom management: Considerations for research to practice. *Education and Treatment of Children, 31*, 351–380.

Snyder, H. (2001). Child delinquents. In L. Loeber & D. P. Farrington (Eds.), *Risk factors and successful interventions*. Thousand Oaks, CA: Sage.

Spilt, J. L., Koomen, H. M., & Jak, S. (2012). Are boys better off with male and girls with female teachers? A multilevel investigation of measurement invariance and gender match in teacher-student relationship quality. *Journal of School Psychology, 50*(3), 363–378.

Stewart, I. (2008). *Why beauty is truth: A history of symmetry*. New York: Basic Books.

Stichter, J. P., Lewis, T. J., Whittaker, T. A., Richter, M., Johnson, N. W., & Trussell, R. P. (2009). Assessing teacher use of opportunities to respond and effective classroom management strategies: Comparisons among high- and low-risk elementary schools. *Journal of Positive Behavior Interventions, 11*, 68–81.

Strain, P. S., & Joseph, G. E. (2004). A not so good job with "good job": A response to Kohn 2001. *Journal of Positive Behavior Interventions, 6*(1), 55–59.

Stronge, J. (2013). *Effective teachers-student achievement: What the research says*. New York: Routledge.

Stronge, J. H., Ward, T. J., & Grant, L. W. (2011). What makes good teachers good? A cross-case analysis of the connection between teacher effectiveness and student achievement. *Journal of Teacher Education, 62*(4), 339–355.

Sutherland, K. S., Alder, N., & Gunter, P. L. (2003). The effect of varying rates of opportunities to respond to academic requests on the classroom behavior of students with EBD. *Journal of Emotional and Behavioral Disorders, 11*(4), 239–248.

Sutherland, K. S., Lewis-Palmer, T., Stichter, J., & Morgan, P. L. (2008). Examining the influence of teacher behavior and classroom context on the behavioral and academic outcomes for students with emotional or behavioral disorders. *Journal of Special Education, 41*(4), 223–233.

Sutherland, K. S., & Wehby, J. H. (2001). Exploring the relationship between increased opportunities to respond to academic requests and the academic and behavioral outcomes of students with EBD: A review. *Remedial and Special Education, 22,* 113–121.

Sutherland, K. S., Wehby, J. H., & Yoder, P. J. (2002). Examination of the relationship between teacher praise and opportunities for students with EBD to respond to academic requests. *Journal of Emotional and Behavioral Disorders, 10,* 5–13.

Takei, Y., & Shouse, R. (2008). Ratings in black and white: Does racial symmetry or asymmetry influence teacher assessment of a pupil's work habits? *Social Psychology of Education, 11*(4), 367–387.

Tapp, J., & Wehby, J. (1995). A multiple option observation system for experimental studies: MOOSES. *Behavior Research Methods, Instruments, & Computers, 27,* 25.

Toldson, I. A., & Lewis, C. W. (2012). Public reciprocity in education for postsecondary success (preps) for students of color: The legal justification and a call for action (editor's commentary). *Journal of Negro Education, 81*(1), 1–9.

Tyson, K. (2003). Notes from the back of the room? Problems and paradoxes in the schooling of young black students. *Sociology of Education. 76,* 326–343. Doi: 10.2307/1519869.

US Department of Education. (2003). *Proven methods: Questions and answers on No Child Left Behind.* Washington DC: Author. Retrieved from http://www.ed.gov/nclb/methods/whatworks/doing.html

US Department of Education, National Center for Education Statistics. (2011). *The digest of education statistics 2010* (NCES 2011-015).

US Department of Education Office of Civil Rights. (2014). *Civil rights data collection: Data snapshot (school discipline).* Issue Brief No. 1. Washington DC: US Department of Education Office for Civil Rights.

Vaughn, S., Gersten, R. L., & Chard, D. J. (2000). The underlying message in LD intervention research: Finding from research syntheses. *Exceptional Children, 67,* 99–114.

Winters, M. A., Haight, R. C., Swaim, T. T., & Pickering, K. A. (2013). The effect of same-gender teacher assignment on student achievement in the elementary and secondary grades: Evidence from panel data. *Economics of Education Review, 34,* 69–75.

About the Authors

Terrance M. Scott, PhD, is a professor, distinguished university scholar, and director of the Center for Instructional and Behavioral Research in Schools at the University of Louisville. He is a former counselor, classroom teacher, and behavior consultant in both residential treatment and public school systems. His research interests include schoolwide prevention systems, the role of instructional variables in managing student behavior, functional behavior assessment/intervention, and scientific research in education.

Regina G. Hirn, PhD, is an assistant professor in the Department of Special Education at the University of Louisville. She is a former classroom teacher, behavior consultant, and assistant director of special education in the public school system. Her research interests include learning strategies for students with learning and behavior disorders and strategies for promoting positive student/teacher interactions during classroom instruction.

Justin T. Cooper, EdD, is an assistant professor of special education at the University of Louisville. He is a former classroom teacher of students with emotional and behavioral disorders in Utah, Wyoming, and Florida. His research interests include examining the effects of teacher behaviors on student behavior in the classroom.

CPSIA information can be obtained
at www.ICGtesting.com
Printed in the USA
BVOW08s0023160317

478643BV00001B/5/P

JESUS,
YOU CAN'T
BE
SERIOUS!

Fully Living the Gospel of Christ

Deacon Glenn
and Linda Harmon

Blessings
Deacon Glenn & Linda

Published by BookLocker.com, Inc., Bradenton, Florida, U.S.A.

Printed on acid-free paper.

BookLocker.com, Inc.
2015

First Edition

Glenn Harmon Ministries
625 Zaharias Circle
Hemet, CA. 92545
337-515-9224

www.glennharmonministries.org
apostlesforjesus@yahoo.com